To Donna—
I am thankful
for your friendship.
Gratefully,

WITH ALL DUE RESPECT

Recovering the Manners & Civility of Political Combat

JEFF COLEMAN

Harrisburg, Pennsylvania

© by Jeff Coleman

All rights reserved. No portion of this book may be reproduced, stored in a retrieval system, or transmitted in any form or by any means—electronic, mechanical, photocopy, recording, scanning, or other—except for brief quotations in critical reviews or articles, without the prior written permission of the author.

Cover design: Scott Cole
Editor: Rachel Stout
Cover image: Getty Images

Published in Mercersburg, Pennsylvania, by Churchill Strategies, LLC.

ISBN: 978-0-9983646-9-8

*"Let your speech be always with grace, seasoned
with salt, that ye may know how ye ought to
answer every man."*

PAUL

CONTENTS

	Foreword by the Hon. R. Norris Clark	i
	Introduction	iv
1.	Humility: The Hon. Peter T. Way	3
2.	Decorum: Mr. Clancy Myer & Mr. Brett O'Donnell	25
3.	Idealism: The Hon. Chad Mayes & The Hon. Dave Reed	49
4.	Truth: Mr. Dan Rather & Mr. Scott Detrow	69
5.	Courage: The Hon. Rick Santorum	97
6.	Solutions: Re-humanizing American Politics & Public Discourse	111
	About the Authors	119
	Sources	121
	Acknowledgements	122

This book is dedicated to my wife,
Rebecca Collins Coleman,
who daily fights the fight of faith with me
for *"a crown of glory that fadeth not away."*

FOREWORD

This book is about our civilization and our civility in public political discourse, and with all due respect to our current politicians, it's needed now more than ever. It's a book for most of us, not just the political actors. It's for the engaged electorate as well as the other half—those who are disengaged due to indifference or disgust.

While the incivility of our last election occasions this book, the issues present in our last election are issues as old as the Republic. In George Washington's second inaugural address, he warned against the dangers of political parties stoked by base partisan spirits. Shortly after his address the factions of Jefferson and Hamilton, North and South, Free and Slave, would be at each other's throats. Throughout our history we've seen great civility contrasted with equally great incivility.

Yet we're becoming manifestly less civil by the minute, both in quality and quantity. New media enables new blows to old codes of conduct. Almost anyone can foster an audience for almost anything, no matter how coarse, false, or fake. Civility makes for boring TV—it no longer sells. Civility, once regarded as a virtue, now appears a vice of weakness.

We need a fresh take on civility and why it should exist in the public square.

Jeff Coleman is perhaps designed by God to write this book. He's a political-actor-turned-communications-professional who listens carefully while drawing out the authentic stories of the causes and companies he represents. For the sake of civility, and for this book, Jeff interviewed outstanding actors from across the political, religious, and cultural spectrum to draw engaging stories that give structure to our political discourse, and new meaning to the well-worn phrase, "with all due respect."

As a family friend and fellow church member who had already served in the Pennsylvania legislature, Jeff counseled my first steps toward elected office. He prepared me for the political consultants who would put words in my mouth while encouraging me to remain real "so my wife would recognize me at the end of the campaign." Years later, when we formed Princeton Strategic Communications, Jeff stepped into the role of creative director. Together, we now counsel a wide range of companies and causes, working with them to effectively tell their own stories.

There was a moment during the last election when this book was born. Public political discourse was becoming the virtual equivalent to video war games, with social media delivering the improvised, explosive devises. Jeff and I have both served in elected office and we regularly serve clients in marketing communications and advocacy, but neither of us could believe what we were witnessing in this new kind of war. We found ourselves asking, "Did they really just say that?"

FOREWORD

This book is fundamentally about our shared story as a nation, as America. As humans, we learn to cooperate through the stories we believe and share with each other. So, our civility rests, tenuously, on the grander story that we all share in our faith. It's the story of all God's children being equally endowed as brothers and sisters, and it explains why we owe our larger human family utmost civility. It is on this foundation that our civilization and our civility rests or falls.

R. Norris Clark

INTRODUCTION

A WINNING EXPERIMENT IN CIVILITY: RUNNING FOR OFFICE

My election to the Pennsylvania House of Representatives in 2000 wasn't supposed to happen. With nearly 70% of voters in my legislative district forming a steel blockade against GOP challengers, Democrats humbled decades of opponents. In the cradle of the United Mine Workers of America, the only available ballot prizes were in the courthouses—Republicans weren't getting anywhere near the elevator to Harrisburg, Pennsylvania or Washington, DC.

When I launched my campaign for state representative as a 25-year-old upstart conservative, the blue wall was beginning to buckle. By the numbers, Western Pennsylvania was the ultimate target-rich environment for Republicans. With two decades of stagnant unemployment combined with rising leftward progressivism, Democrats were abandoning their country music wing.

Campaigning for state representative was one of the richest experiences of my life. The 60th Legislative District was a beautiful, hilly patchwork of first- and second-generation immigrant families whose lives were still deeply connected to their churches, social clubs, and

INTRODUCTION

summertime festivals. By the time I arrived, all but a few factories were torn down, and those remaining were slowly being dismantled.

Despite living in the shadow of economic death, the people I met in this region were some of the most loving, trusting people I have ever known. They introduced me to the culinary wonders of haluski and halupka, and those incredible buckets of handmade pierogies from the old Ukrainian church in Ford City. They treated me—the transplanted son of Presbyterian missionary parents, a guy who had never played high school football and couldn't trace his lineage through Ellis Island—as a member of their family. More importantly, when they learned I was a Republican, only a fraction refrained from hospitality.

As the no-name challenger to a five-term incumbent, I was holding the political equivalent of a slingshot with a little less than five smooth stones. The local gazette's front-page profile called ours the "David versus Goliath" campaign. Everyone knew the outcome—I would lose, and likely lose big.

But God had other plans. In the year Al Gore and George W. Bush were tossed into overtime, my political education would move from political theory to personal reality in a single day. In one of two GOP pickups in the State House that year, my race—eked out by a few hundred votes—helped return House Republicans to the majority. As its youngest member, I became the Cinderella of the hour.

THE TOWN OF APOLLO

As a teenager living in my adopted hometown of Apollo, Pennsylvania, I learned the ways of my future profession by chasing down anyone with the thinnest connection to politics who passed through our little borough. Our town was a rugged river community best known for its annual Moon Landing Celebration and its former nuclear submarine fuel facility with a dubious cleanup history.

Not many families were moving to Apollo in the late 80s. What had once been a respectable, middle-class steel town with dozens of active churches, a handful of movie theaters, and every flavor of fraternal club, was now in the throes of a torturous transition. It had plenty of tenacity, but its leaders and citizens could not agree on a forward direction.

Apollo was traditionally a Democratic town, and within a few years, Democrats traded their workingman constituencies for a different class of activist voter—a far more socially liberal voter that hailed almost exclusively from urban and suburban zip codes. It's a shift that would later drive tens of thousands into the ranks of Tea Party, Sarah Palin, and Donald Trump populism.

INTRODUCTION

REPUBLICANS TAKE AIM AND MISS

For consultants, the problem with demographic trends is that they don't tell you much about the idiosyncrasies of voters. Data doesn't measure how cynical or joyful a community might be at a particular moment in history. It doesn't tell you how willing they'll be to break a habit of straight party voting, and it never reveals what kind of candidate has the right blend of a personal and political story to make a convincing case for something new.

In the late 1980s, not everyone was caught flatfooted with the potential for mass Democratic migration. Some saw fissures on issues like abortion, gun control, taxes, and law and order. As Philadelphia liberals tilted left, Pittsburgh's conservative Democrats began to look for a new home. This is when Republicans began to look west.

In 1989, Democratic state Representative Henry Livengood died, and Republicans recruited Jim Scahill. If there was ever a chance to beat a Democrat in a Democratic seat, this was the year, and Jim was the man. This campaign would create a positive case for the candidate and, with the assistance of opposition research, create a negative counter-narrative against the opponent. In local politics, this level of sophisticated attack was brand new.

Republicans made Scahill heroically pro-gun, pro-life, and pro-coal. The Democrat, Tim Pesci, would be painted suspect on virtually every issue, even with nearly identical public policy positions on issues including guns and abortion.

In an environment where candidates did little more than pass out nail files and matchbooks at county fairs, this kind of approach turned the expected gentleman's contest into a divisive bloodbath. In the closing days of the campaign, with polls showing Scahill in the hunt, an early morning misfire with an automated call from Senator John Heinz confirmed suspicions that outsiders and special interests were pulling strings. This was all Democrats needed to win.

OUR RULES OF CIVILITY

By the time I was ready to run against Mr. Pesci, I was convinced of the need for a different kind of campaign. We would use data to identify likely voters, but instead of aiming different messages at subgroups and niche issues, we'd express the same message to everyone. Our strategy rested on a hunch that voters had begun to resent the carnival tricks that had invaded local politics.

Whenever a reporter or microphone was nearby, I'd repeat the vow against negative campaigning. At every stop, I would predict future attacks by the defenders of "old politics." By the end, Representative Pesci was annoyed enough to start calling me "Jeffy" in public debates, and any evidence of momentum won me a mild at-

INTRODUCTION

tack-mailer in the closing days of the campaign. By then, the genuine relationship I had with voters was a chord not easily severed.

At this point, it might be helpful to review the practical ways our campaign messaging differed from most:

> 1. Always refer to our opponent as "Representative Pesci"—honoring his public service, while gently reminding voters he was the incumbent.
>
> 2. Repeat the same message at every door and every public event. A campaign with limited funds would need every possible bit of repetition to fuel our message.
>
> 3. On issues where Mr. Pesci and I agreed, exhibit greater passion and conviction. Incumbents tend to play the big issues safe and quiet.
>
> 4. Remind voters to "vote the person, not the party." Voters believe they're more independent than their voting records indicate.
>
> 5. Emphasize the fact that we are running a positive, issues-oriented campaign. Engage in no negative or misleading campaigning against my opponent.

6. Provide a sincere answer to the reason for the campaign. Voters need to understand a candidate's motives.

7. Engage the voter's most difficult and controversial issues immediately.

Looking back on that year, I know why Representative Pesci would call our campaign volunteers "The Children of the Corn" in his post-defeat farewell speech. Instead of taking him on with the drums and trumpets of an advancing army, we treated the individual voter encounter as a unique event, with each more significant than any other.

On November 7, 2000, our experiment in civility won with 52% of the vote, scaling a massive 2:1 voter registration and spending deficit, and overcoming an incumbent who had never lost an election. We realized our hope of running an elevated, respectful campaign, but we did not reorder the direction of politics.

As I write this book in the days just before the end of the bitterest year in modern American history, the campaign to recover the manners and civility of political discourse has only begun.

In the closing months of 2016, I started a small conversation on my Facebook page to see if others shared the view that our personal and national conversation was precariously close to destroying the

INTRODUCTION

framework of American civility. Would the values of American public discourse be lost or permanently damaged if we didn't moderate our approach or disqualify those who refused to embrace the norms of civility?

While some of my online friends saw danger in the unfiltered, salacious style of this year's campaign, many believed it was just a blip, an anomaly. Others reminded me of the duels, brawls, and wildly partisan press that are the forgotten companions of all the founder's high-minded idealism. There never was an era of civility.

I concede that in many ways, they are right. Every period in our national life is an example of greatness mixed with petulance, and 2016 was no exception. But I am not prepared to accept the idea that 2016 was or is our future. There has to be more.

In this book, I took these same questions to a collection of friends and professional associates who held well-formed opinions about the way things were and ought to be. They hail from the communities of journalism, government, academia, military, and faith, and answer my questions in ways I never expected.

My hope is that this little book and the people you'll meet on its pages will encourage you to expect more from those privileged to earn your vote.

WITH ALL DUE RESPECT

Hon. Peter T. Way, Photographer: Joel Coleman

Kristi Way, Photographer: Joel Coleman

"Sense shines with a double luster when it is set in humility. An able and yet humble man is a jewel worth a kingdom."

WILLIAM PENN

"Every action done in company, ought to be with some sign of respect, to those that are present."

GEORGE WASHINGTON,
RULES OF CIVILITY

CHAPTER ONE

HUMILITY

Hon. Peter T. Way, Pastor and Former Virginia Lawmaker

Before I introduce you to this remarkable friend of mine, you need to know this chapter is not a scolding—far from it. It's not a moralizing rant about why we shouldn't elect arrogant people to be president or prevent ambitious dreamers from trying to correct our biggest public problems. This book is also not an obituary of forgotten Puritan virtues.

This little book is a request for its readers to reconsider the value of meekness and humility in public life. It's a call to recognize those who don't automatically crave applause or seek personal legacy. It's a plea to those who are quiet, reflective, measured, kind, and gracious to bring their balancing virtues to our public debate.

In May 2016, Gallup polled the leadership traits behind the public's support for the four leading presidential candidates. The candidates' strongest attributes were considered in this poll, which both

HUMILITY

revealed the reason for their appeal to voters and mirrored our culture's momentary understanding of presidential leadership.

Here's the list that was compiled and tested for the survey: intense, competitive, inspiring, courageous, prepared, consistent, enthusiastic, cares about individuals, emphasizes success, analytical, focused, and visionary.

The poll presented the strong image narratives of Clinton, Sanders, Cruz, and Trump. Like most modern candidacies, their campaigns designed the candidate messages to satisfy audience tastes.

Clinton's message was for the mainstream, Democratic establishment. Bernie Sanders was betting on the affections of young progressives, intellectual liberals and the disenfranchised. Cruz and Trump seemed to be casting their nets for the same constituency: a new mega-majority of non-establishment Republicans.

For modern politicians, consumer (voter) data is king. Thus, the Gallup list reads like a high school career aptitude test. Would a student be better as a greeter or a salesman? Should he pursue a degree in counseling or computer programming? Would she be more likely to succeed in retail or research?

Every speech, TV spot, post, tweet, and interview reinforces a self-designed image that is ready-made for its intended audience. This year, as favored candidates fell, voters seemed to be ranking and re-ranking their new candidate's winning attributes.

Read the list again. This time, look for what's missing. Are there any attributes, other than courage, that suggested we were choosing a leader based on anything other than surface qualities? Can the hiring of a speech coach or image consultant offset every perceived deficiency? Before the court of public opinion, none of those leadership attributes are out of reach for a determined candidate.

If the list can be trusted, voters in 2016 were looking for coaching and cheerleading qualities, not the presidential traits of someone we would want on Mount Rushmore. Succeeding as a candidate is predicated merely on convincingly playing the part of a leader.

Here's the point. The old standards and tests of leadership revealed the sturdiness and reliability of a person under pressure. The character of a candidate was the complex puzzle of virtues that made one increasingly reliable and ready for greater responsibilities. It is the hard trials that prepare men and women for higher levels of service. Leaders who possess character are seen to exhibit a wisdom and maturity that, over time, are revealed in greater measure.

Today's standards position the leader at the beginning of an hour-long episode. Every day a politician can adjust personality traits to stabilize rating hiccups and overnight anomalies. Advertisers (contributors) renew for another season (term), and the show (politician) avoids cancellation.

In this way, a candidate's record versus promises becomes irrelevant to the final decision to elect or re-elect. When a candidate's bad decisions damage polling, campaigns schedule photo ops and town hall meetings to demonstrate miraculous personal growth. Time and money correct the candidate's deficiencies within the span of a few hours.

The problem should be obvious. The candidate, who regularly recasts his personal and political image to win the election, will also likely undergo a continual metamorphosis once elected.

Is this brazen lack of character a problem? Does it matter? Can anyone win and hold the voter's affections without undergoing a little political nip and tuck?

I hope you're still with me. These questions speak to the heart of the decision we made in this year's presidential election, and this won't be the last time they will need to be asked. Should character—defined as predictable consistency in private and personal behavior—still count?

It should count, and it does count. It counts because in the relatively short time between Watergate and the Trump inauguration, we've shredded the list of disqualifying character deficiencies that brought down the presidency of Richard Nixon. We've replaced it with a set of rules that prizes fuzzy ideas of authenticity over the reliability of personal character.

HUMILITY: CIVILITY'S CORNERSTONE

Humility was once the crown jewel of America's political virtues, and it has been perfectly expressed in human history only once. In the realm of leadership traits, humility was the high score in the carnival game with the sledgehammer and big bell. Achieving true humility is rare, and it's doubly impossible to maintain. Still, until recently, we expected leaders to swing hard and occasionally ring the bell.

No candidate or officeholder has ever been a flawless practitioner, and for every act of humility, there seems to be a large offset—a reminder that it's never going to be a permanent strand of the DNA. Maybe it's a fiery temper or a closet full of indulgent, selfish indiscretions. Pride lurks at every corner.

It takes less than a minute to unravel a lifetime of good deeds. For example, when Congressman Patrick Kennedy snapped at airport security and for days headlined the evening news. Or the moment when Congressman Joe Wilson jarred the pageantry of a state-of-the-union address by calling the president a liar. Pride is 100% bipartisan.

My catalog of pride-fueled hypocrisies is well known to many reading this book. If you don't believe me, let's talk.

Until recently, politicians needed to at least feign modesty or selflessness. Intertwined with the idea of public service is a belief that subordinating vanities and ambitions were essential to being worthy of trust.

HUMILITY

Humility is the traffic cop in the center of the public square. It keeps hard-driving egos from the bedlam of multi-care pileups. Humility is deferential, putting the agendas of others before its own. It yields, stops, waits, and listens before making its play.

When humility dissolved during the GOP presidential primary debates, the resulting mayhem was a legendary example of why civility cannot happen without this regulating force. Millions of us watched the unchecked carnage of those debates in slow, agonizing motion. It was ugly.

So, if you agree but think I'm teetering toward a Pollyannaish notion of political combat, there's someone I think you should meet. My friend, Peter Way, is someone who survived a difficult upbringing to take on a series of assignments bigger than his pedigree or station. Fair warning: out of humility, he would never agree with the assertions I'm about to make regarding his character.

MEET PETER WAY

Peter Way would never consider himself a living lesson in humility. Like most in his generation, he's unfamiliar with the phenomenon of styling achievements or virtues into a personal brand, and he's never learned the art of the "humble brag." It's widely understood among his family that with limited knowledge about his emergency car flip phone, Peter Way will never be posting on Facebook or Instagram.

He's not perfect, but to him, self-elevation is almost inconceivable.

In Way's world, there's an urgency of duty that leaves no room for daydreams or distractions. There's work to do, and he will do it.

Peter Way doesn't mock our 21st-century lives, which often appear more virtual than real, but to him, social media isn't a substitute for community. While he hasn't adjusted his life to new technologies, neither does he cling to a nostalgia for the less complicated communication of typewriters and handwritten letters.

Way holds to the conviction that circumstances are not self-directed. In fact, he would say that they're out of our hands altogether. It is because of this that life is not about escaping difficulties such as death, disease, and unemployment, but is rather about finding purpose and redemption in these trials.

This is the manner of life for many in Peter Way's generation—a call of duty often detoured by the harsh, unexplained blows of Providence. It's about planning a course but never allowing ambition to get in the way of serving wherever life takes you. Trials serve as gateways to a deeper faith. Our charge is to wait or move forward with determined energy. The outcomes are God's alone.

Way is gifted with a booming baritone speaking voice and stands a tad over six feet. Battered by ugly tangles with stomach cancer and lymphoma, his body has endured ample physical suffering. Once weighing a lean one hundred seventy pounds, the medical arsenal used to keep him alive has stripped away at least forty. He is tall and skinny in a way that signals the presence of a quiet, relentless torture.

The voice, smile, and happy blue eyes are all there, but the great man standing is a shadow of his former self. The timber of mind and character remain unchanged, but the body is slowly bowing to his enemy—cancer.

In nearly every observable area of his long life, Peter Way seems oblivious to daily anxieties. While he directs anger at injustices in politics or football, his reaction is never mean or personal. Somehow his understanding of human frailty subdues these potential responses. Disappointment is never assigned a name or a face.

PETER THE PREACHER

In the weeks leading up to the 2016 presidential election, I made the three-hour drive south to Brandy Station, Virginia, to hear Reverend Peter Way preach the morning sermon at Christ Episcopal Church.

The woman and her husband seated in the row ahead told me how the Union Army once dismantled the church for coffins. Later, the church would win a post-war reparations appeal from the federal government to rebuild. Each year during observances of the Battle of Brandy Station, the congregation of less than seventy-five holds a worship service on the remains of its original foundation.

WITH ALL DUE RESPECT

When Way accepted the posting at Christ Church less than twelve years ago, the church had dwindled to fifteen attendees. The new preacher's reputation for simple, engaging Bible teaching and a shepherd's heart soon packed out the tiny sanctuary.

On the morning of my visit, I met him at the church a half hour before the service. I'd known Reverend Way during my college years at Liberty through my wife's best friend—his daughter Kristi. Back then he was a legend; today he's a role model. Through the nasty fog of this year's national drama, I wanted some clarity from him.

He greeted me at the church in khakis and green flannel. Peter Way isn't fussy; he half grumbles about putting on "all this stuff," referring to the white cassock required by church order. He knows every word of the liturgy by heart, racing through sections, somehow not diluting its majesty. At any speed, his God-like voice demands attention.

"Tough stuff," he warns the congregation about the day's sermon. He reads the words of Joshua spoken to the children of Israel: "Choose you this day who you will serve."

Throughout his brief sermon, he reminds listeners of the challenge of carrying out this mandate. It is never easy. Following Jesus and denying ourselves—the Christian life itself—isn't our natural inclination.

Everything about Peter Way's life is supernatural.

During the week, he drives himself to chemotherapy. He's the one who shops and cares for his wife, Elizabeth, in the throes of increasingly distant days and nights due to her memory loss. Most recently, he's also taken in a brother—a Korean War vet plagued by war-induced hearing loss, congestive heart failure, and Parkinson's. The weekly duties at Christ Church require another burden—an hour-long, one-way commute from his home near Charlottesville.

He tells none of this to me, and his congregation doesn't know the depth of their pastor's health trials. His sense of duty wouldn't allow the transfer of his burdens to others. His duty is to lighten loads, not add to them.

PETER THE HEADMASTER

The early 1960s reveal a trove of clues to Way's long journey toward the kind of humility and self-denial that would later serve him well in public life. Before there was a church or, I suspect, even the prospect of donning the collar, there was a home for boys—its name, Tros-dale, imaginatively repurposed from his middle name. Ahead of its time for rural Virginia, the home was racially integrated, structured, and distinctly Christian.

Tros-dale's origins are indeed remarkable. In 1961, when the boys' school where Way was teaching closed, the state found a suitable home for all but two of the displaced youths. Drawing from a modest inheritance from his stepfather, Way bought a house and established Tros-dale, telling a reporter for *The Daily Progress* in 1968 that "the boys must move in and take part in the community just as much as any other child—if they're going to grow up to be good citizens. I try to stress that we live up to our responsibilities."

His goal was to give the boys something that had eluded him for much of his childhood—the chance to fit in. From church attendance to Boy Scouts and Little League, Tros-dale's residents would receive the incalculable gift of an ordinary upbringing.

Over decades, Way and his wife used their sprawling home, on a pastoral setting in Albemarle County, Virginia, to house dozens of young men placed in the state's foster system. The Ways' pioneering approach to caring for these boys saved them from the black hole of institutional care.

A combination of factors flowing from his parent's divorce and a series of significant moves in early life were critical to forming Way's management of his home. Instead of harsh, authoritarian discipline, Way modeled a soft, humor-filled demeanor that nudged even the most contrarian boys back within house rules.

Despite the nobility of its mission, Tros-dale persisted through adversity on many fronts, although most were brought on by government bureaucracy. State regulators repeatedly stepped in, citing the need for changes like institutional record keeping and costly modifications. What may have been sound policy to an office-bound welfare regulator seemed like the beginning of the end to Way.

Even the centerpiece of Tros-dale's living experience, the expansive dining room table, became a sore point for regulators, Way recalls with some laughter. Regulators cited new studies that allegedly proved that smaller, restaurant-like tables facilitate better conversation than traditional, rectangular tables. The Ways' dining room table wasn't compliant.

Beyond government intervention, acceptance of another kind eluded the boys at Tros-dale. Well into the 1980s, the spectacle of a white family living with African-American children caused consternation for some neighbors. Kristi recalls the longstanding ban on her entire family from community pool membership, even though the pool literally overlapped the Way's property line. The reason for the slight was apparent. By the time the ban was lifted, the Ways had installed their own swimming pool.

PETER THE LAWMAKER

Like his path to the clergy, Way's journey to the Virginia General Assembly wasn't the result of meticulous planning. Providence propelled him far beyond resources or resume.

Way's decision to enter politics was fueled by one of his encounters with governmental and educational regulators in the administration of Tros-dale. As a non-partisan, somewhat naïve combatant, he decided to challenge a sitting member of the Albemarle County Board of Supervisors.

In 1968, the tentacles of The Byrd Organization, the statewide infrastructure of Virginia's former Governor and U.S. Senator Harry Byrd, were still gatekeepers at all levels of government. The Democratic Byrd Organization, impassioned to block school racial integration, fought to hold seats on supervisory boards that maintained jurisdiction over county school systems. People like Peter Way wouldn't remain unnoticed.

When he dropped by the county clerk's office to file as an independent candidate, the staff couldn't find the forms for a non-Democrat. Challenges to the machine were rare. Undeterred, he traveled to Richmond to begin the process of putting his name on the ballot.

Unaware of the opposition's considerable power, he launched his campaign with a peppy slogan: "Make Way for Supervisor." The thirty-year-old political neophyte walked straight into the teeth of the old lion's machine. On Election Day, he shocked the system and himself by winning an astonishing 52% of the vote.

"I was horrified," he said.

After a single term in office, he'd had enough. "Being on the board of supervisors drove me to the seminary," he said.

After a short hiatus, he would re-enter public service, accepting an appointment to the school board and winning back a seat on the board of supervisors. He later became its chairman. By the next time he ran, The Byrd Organization's influence had nearly disappeared. Virginia was leaving behind some of its more painful controversies, and Peter Way was on the right side of emerging history.

In 1991, with Tros-dale collapsing under the weight of regulations, a new opportunity arrived to pull government back within its natural borders. When future Virginia Governor George Allen vacated his seat in the Virginia House of Delegates, a position once held by Thomas Jefferson, the duty fell to Way to keep it in Republican hands.

But partisan loyalty wasn't much of a motivator to run for higher office. Way viscerally detests party divisions and expectations. As a supervisor, he "never, ever" remembers the six-member panel playing party games. They operated as a non-partisan body.

The triggering event for his candidacy was far more inspired.

When state inspectors turned on Babe, Tros-dale's three-gallon-a-day milk cow, it was the proverbial last straw. For the cow once dubbed "a legend in her time" by the local newspaper, even the purchase of a home pasteurizer wouldn't satisfy the inflexible regulations on her milk production. The government said the cow had to go.

"That cow was one of the things that propelled me to run for the state legislature," he says with some well-placed indignation. Babe was now the poster cow for government overreach and foolishness.

On election night, the contest resulted in a tie vote between Way and his Democratic opponent. By day's end, election officials found an apparently missing ballot tipping the contest to Way's opponent by a single vote.

Recalling the race, he remembers the courtesies he and his opponent exchanged during months of campaigning. No negative attacks. No misleading mailers. They entered and ended the race as friends.

During a dramatic pre-Christmas recount, election officials determined that human error recorded a "9" as "0," erasing seven votes from the winner's tally. This meant that Way won his first election to the House of Delegates by single digits.

Once again, political observers in Virginia were stunned. The day he arrived, his opponent's name was already applied to the office door when Delegate-elect Way came to work in the stately white building that once served as the Capitol of the Confederacy.

"When I went to the legislature, I was totally shocked," Way said. It was his first real encounter with a political culture dominated by partisanship.

One party rule immediately sank his chances for effectiveness on passion points like welfare reform. The Speaker from the opposing party allowed no space on committees where the freshman's expertise on foster care could matter. His seat assignment in the back row of the chamber and membership in the minority party made him feel especially outclassed.

"I was scared to death," he recalled meekly of his first days in Richmond. "You never think you're going to be prepared for all of this."

For Delegate Way, frustration led to focusing on reforming the legislature itself. Famously part-time and modestly compensated, the pomp and prestige were still enough to make the State Capitol a petri dish for corruption.

"It's just appalling to me the way incumbency leads to power and corruption," he thunders. "When we are in Richmond, we are treated as gods. People live that way all year long. Eventually you get to think you are that good."

Perhaps Peter Way's view of original sin and human nature informed the way he saw the corruptibility of colleagues. He knew that power would generally overtake even the best men and women. Reforming the rules of the House of Delegates was as necessary as clearing out an alcoholic's liquor cabinet.

When it came time for his first budget vote, he joined a pair of future Republican stars—Delegate Bob McDonnell, a future governor, and Eric Cantor, an eventual Majority Leader in Congress—in being the lonely trio to oppose the spending package. It was a pattern he'd frequently repeat.

During three terms in office, he quietly voted against all but one state budget. Despite the need to scrap for every vote, Governor Allen affirmed his friend's principled independence on GOP spending plans. "I think you did the right thing," the independent lawmaker remembers the governor saying. Once again, friendship was protected by principle.

When Way retired from the General Assembly in 1997, he kept a promise to limit his time in office. His dream of imposing universal limits on legislative service went completely unrealized.

FAILURE OR SUCCESS?

What should we make of Peter Way's nearly imperceptible exit from public service and seemingly invisible record of accomplishment? His time in office doesn't yield much when it's Googled, and his Wikipedia page isn't even complete.

To some, occupying a legislative seat without wall trophies, or at least the minor glory of naming rights to a community center, doesn't mean much.

What's the point of running if you aren't there to make a difference or notch good deeds into the public record? If you fail to promote your legacy by acting as its prime interpreter, who will?

For Way, it's never been a dilemma. Duty isn't self-seeking. His responsibilities like caring for Elizabeth or tending to his Sunday morning flock aren't performed for the sake of heroism. Running for public office, in his mind, was a temporary assignment. The call to be a pastor, husband, and father is permanent.

HUMILITY

I believe Peter Way's life is a heroic success because he was faithful in what most consider the little things. With ego in check and a piercing awareness of his imperfections, he never became a braggart. His voice had volume, but he was never a loudmouth.

Men and women of Peter Way's stock are the consciences of the places they serve. They know the stories of hundreds of people around them—the people who often go unnoticed by the power brokers and political climbers.

Without the grace and humility of those like Peter Way, the public square is a calculating and uncaring place. When those driven by selfish ambition overpower voices like his, the most vulnerable citizens lose their advocates.

Yes, the meeker and milder public servants rarely produce a gallery of noteworthy public achievements or notice, but their personal influence on the people and institutions they serve is a far more enduring legacy.

Blessed are the meek.

Civility begins with humility.

Humility recognizes the limits of any personality, party, or legislative body.

Humility places the person opposite in higher esteem.

Humility draws the line that says: "I'll engage you in a battle of ideas, but I'll never say or do anything to poison another's view of your character or motives."

Humility says someone created in God's image is worthy of honor and protection.

Humility tempers the fires of a moment with a wider view.

Clancy Myer, Photographer: Bill Crawford

Brett O'Donnell, Photographer: Joel Coleman

"We cannot learn from one another until we stop shouting at one another, until we speak quietly enough so that our words can be heard as well as our voices . . ."

RICHARD NIXON

CHAPTER TWO

DECORUM

Clancy Myer, Parliamentarian, Pennsylvania House of Representatives
Brett O'Donnell, Presidential Debate Coach and Campaign Advisor

In the closing days of the presidential campaign, raucous, fist-raised crowds extended as far as the eye could see. Crushing crowds surrounded his motorcade in every town he visited. Dismissed as a regional candidate, he was only expected to win the deep south, but with no prospect of growing support beyond the undereducated and working poor.

His self-styled profile was that of a straight-arrow, incorruptible outsider, but his lifestyle was more king-like than populist. When campaigning in rural areas, dramatic helicopter arrivals added to his overall white knight mystique. When details about personal finances dribbled out and watchdog reporters hovered over apparent inconsistencies, he waved away every allegation. He would never allow any report to undermine the winning reformist brand he'd created for himself. When they punched, he counterpunched with glib sarcasm and mockery. Like a Teflon™ pan, the hotter the fire, the less anything seemed to stick.

His stance was defiant and anti-establishment, at times vulgar and almost always irreverent. His campaign promises were outrageous and ungrounded to detractors but sounded like inspired prose to growing legions of supporters. To them, he was the embodiment of hope.

Even straight-laced evangelical Christians fell in love with his repeated pledge to restore law and order. In communities ravaged by drug addiction and poverty, still suffering the loss of long-gone industries, nothing about his non-traditional personal life or irreverent, profanity-laced speeches had any noticeable effect.

As his polls soared, the media scoured the record for hints of a governing approach, but other than his long-winded speeches and equally entertaining interviews, they were unable to link him to any political philosophy or leadership model.

Supporters too defied stereotypes. Each segment of the massive electoral coalition seemed to hear their political song sung exactly the way they needed to hear it. Their candidate was the fulfillment of so many different meanings of the notion of hope.

The presidential election of 2016 would be embarrassing and cruel to each of his well-prepared opponents. Even though many of them were well rehearsed for their presidential audition, he was the man of the moment. The carefully crafted, packaged messaging and choreographed rallies of his opposition only reminded voters that politics has always been just a show. They had celebrities and the media; he had the people.

In the closing weeks of the campaign, even misogynistic comments about women did nothing to slow momentum. It wasn't even close.

On Monday, May 9, 2016, the man nicknamed the "Donald Trump of Asia," Rodrigo Duterte, surged past the incumbent's handpicked successor, the daughter of a leading actor, and the sitting vice president, to win a sixteen-point victory in the Philippine presidential election.

The establishment of this Asian archipelago was reeling. The new president had broken every unstated rule of political decorum. In a political split-second, old world civility had taken a near-fatal blow.

In the Philippines, the first months of Duterte's six-year term have been unnervingly chaotic for world observers. The provocateur's campaign style became his governing mantra. In less than six months, the new president nearly upended the historic alliance with the United States, flirted with the region's communist giant, China, and cheered thousands of vigilante-style killings of suspected drug addicts and dealers.

Just as President Donald Trump warms America's relationship with Russia via Tweet exchanges with Vladimir Putin, Duterte received a red-carpet welcome from Chinese President Xi Jinping.

In the hours after Trump's electoral victory, Rodrigo Duterte was one of a handful of world leaders to immediately issue effusive praise for his new friend. After months of publicly attacking America, from its ambassador to President Obama, Duterte issued an almost giddy reversal: "We both curse. For any small reason, we curse. We are kind of similar."

"JUST GETTING REAL"

Where's the connection? How is the Philippine election instructive for the American experience? Developing nations like the Philippines always seem to flip from stability to chaos without warning. Like in Venezuela, Egypt, and many other personality-driven cultures, poverty breeds opportunities for the strongman. Aren't these cultures naturally attracted to indecorous, freewheeling dictators?

Add to this the historical fact that American institutions are older and far more durable. We are the grandfather of the entire idea of constitutional government. We're not some banana republic. And wasn't it Jefferson who wrote something about the need for "a little rebellion now and then" to rattle the stale traditions and keep democracy vibrant?

The 2016 election in the Philippines is instructive beyond obvious personality comparisons and shocking outcomes. It represents a yearning by democracies young and old to burn the script.

In the spirit of the moment, the measured, think-before-speaking politician is a counterfeit messenger, a puppet for a host of shadowy interest groups and party bosses. Better to have the stream-of-conscience leadership of nonconformists like Donald Trump or Rodrigo Duterte than to grant power to the political elites.

Before 2016, there was already a wider, restless culture demanding release from the prison of censored tongues and normal lifestyles. From commercially dependent nightly newscasts to sitcoms with laugh tracks, these streams of seemingly endless revenue gave way to the revolution of "unscripted" TV.

In 1992, I was one of the millions of teenagers who watched the first episode of MTV's groundbreaking reality show *The Real World*. In the show's opening sequence, the announcer introduced the episode with the following premise:

"This is the true story of seven strangers, picked to live in a loft, live together, and have their lives taped, to find out what happens when people stop being polite and start getting real."

The show delivered the seismic shift it promised, forcing a full-scale market revolution of the entire television medium. The Big Three newscasts ceded generations of viewers to 24-hour infotainment channels like Fox News and MSNBC. Long-running comedies and formula-driven dramas faced a reinvent-or-die moment. Most died.

NBC launched *The Apprentice* in 2004, connecting with audiences who complained that the reality show genre had grown intolerably flat. By turning to one of Manhattan's iconic 1980s tabloid stars, and populating his supporting cast with young, serious-minded professionals, NBC had its new hook. *The Apprentice* was a step above the premise of the vapid celebrity house or trapped-on-an-island genres because each episode held the promise of business insights from one of the world's most successful and cunning dealmakers.

For a hungry, success-driven culture, Donald Trump was granting the equivalent of weekly golden tickets. Complex problems were resolved within a single episode, while the weakest of the pack suffered a humiliating cab ride to the airport. Only one man, Donald J. Trump, was free from researchers and shareholders. In full command, he made decisions and granted wishes for whom he chose.

Ironically, it's the formula of this show that made it easy for over half of America to forget Trump the reality show star and casino mogul and instead visualize him as a president, negotiating on a grander scale.

If one man could single-handedly spot the flaws in a fledging startup, or pick the one entrepreneurial talent in a field of duds, then why would the old rules apply to him? To many Americans, the niceties of decorum and political manners appear antithetical to the success of men like Trump. "Whatever it takes" and "by any means necessary" are the slogans of real winners. Who needs manners?

WITH ALL DUE RESPECT

DECORUM'S LONGTIME ALLY: PARLIAMENTARIAN CLANCY MYER

When I arrived at the question of rules for public discourse, I approached it practically, turning to a man who sits in the control tower of the Pennsylvania House of Representatives, the rostrum. In the House chamber, the rostrum is perched high above the heads of rank-and-file members, but well below the great public gallery of narrow, theatre-style seating positioned opposite the Speaker. This space is the parliamentarian's command post when the General Assembly is in session.

First installed as the parliamentarian in 1978, Clancy Myer has been the trusted whisperer-in-chief to Speakers of both parties. His appointment by K. Leroy Irvis, the nation's first African-American Speaker of any state legislature since Reconstruction, was a special honor. Irvis was known as a brilliant, extemporaneous debater whom Myer described as deeply spiritual and a stickler for order. "Everyone who knew him would say he was the finest orator this House has ever experienced. He would hold the House spellbound with no preparation at all."

Decorum in the Irvis years was essential to preserving the debate. Myer recalls that Irvis "broke numerous gavels" to maintain order. The former teacher often told members, "You're acting like school children," to shame them into observing the House rules.

"He expected better behavior out of them," said Myer.

In the years before cameras were permitted to broadcast proceedings, this kind of accountability was necessary to keep rowdy sessions from becoming a useless waste of the public's time and dime. Permanent cameras didn't arrive in the House until the 1990s. "There was no playing to the cameras," says Myer. It was on the speaker, parliamentarian, and sergeant at arms to keep order.

For Clancy Myer, learning the ropes of professional civility from one of its storied practitioners was a fortunate start to a long career. Today, with centuries of precedent available at nearly instant recall, and a rare mastery of the official rules of the body, he's easily the most respected member of the institutional team that supports House members. Years of serving House Speakers with varying temperaments and training have given him a mental catalog. He knows how the rules should or, more importantly, should not be used in the thick of floor combat.

In the House, Clancy Myer has no microphone to address members directly. His words are rarely contradicted in official rulings, and go unfiltered to the ear of the House Speaker, not the wider body. While his words aren't law, they are the opinions that guide most of the decisions made from the chair. As de facto consigliere, he bears the burden of keeping the boisterous legislative body focused on the matter at hand.

FIST FIGHTS & ALCOHOL

Like most longtime observers of American legislative bodies from Congress to the states, Clancy Myer has no fantasies about the way things used to be in his chamber. The thick glass was installed separating members on the House floor from their constituents in the gallery because of objects occasionally rained down on lawmakers from irritated observers.

When I arrived, the stories had morphed into rumors that gunfire from the gallery precipitated the addition of a bulletproof barrier. Myer says there is nothing to confirm this version of the story, but there have been fistfights and other interruptions of good order. In an era past, when catering dollars were easier to come by, late-night, alcohol-fueled dinners unleashed the lesser angels of disorder.

Apart from members' less-than-decorous behavior, the real enemy of formal civility inside the legislative body is the coveting of the other party's seats. According to Myer, the new way caucuses target the opposing party's members for defeat has dramatically changed the tone and tenor of public debate.

Until the early 1990s, a gentleman's agreement existed between Republican and Democratic House leaders. This agreement stated that a lawmaker's public voting record was within bounds for campaign contrasts, but easily misconstrued legislative expenses and reimbursements were not legitimate grounds for attack.

While we didn't discuss who broke the agreement, the tactic of labeling Democratic incumbents as opportunists eating from the public trough was certainly one of the reasons for the GOP's string of successes that began in the early 2000s. The reality is that both parties equally benefit from a culture of self-aggrandizement and perks.

When campaigns between caucuses turn personal outside the Capitol, the likelihood of forging deep, bi-partisan bonds of friendship, and more importantly, legislative cooperation, becomes a vanishing prospect. Politics, like the rest of life, survives on trust and respect.

"I could never conceive to be running for office today with what people have to go through to be elected," laments Myer. "It's no wonder we look bad in the public's eye. We paint ourselves that way."

THOMAS JEFFERSON STILL RULES THE HOUSE

The worldwide rejection of established order and institutions is for many a refreshing embrace of authenticity. A speech is often deemed calculated or the intellectual product of an advisor when it's read from a teleprompter. Instantaneous reaction to national or world events is often a bigger story than the substance of the response itself. Every norm in public communication and debate is under review to decide where efficiency should overtake centuries of tradition. Measured, thorough, and accurate responses are increasingly less important than the optics of the real-time, decisive leader.

It's inevitable that these outside changes will begin to affect how the public views the seemingly arcane language employed during state legislative and congressional proceedings.

Why wouldn't the people's business be conducted in the no-frills, fast-paced style of *American Idol* or *America's Got Talent*? Why do legislators still drive hours to cast an in-person ballot when the technology exists for at-home, remote voting? And why can't lawmakers debate without the constraint of centuries-old rules that squelch spontaneity and emotion? Can't decision making on a public issue just be real?

I posed this premise to the parliamentary veteran during a visit to his office in the State Capitol. While Myer answers somewhat predictably, saying "I like the tradition," he concedes that some of the processes have already been trending toward a more relaxed banter than the traditional form of debate where members posed questions through the Speaker.

In the process of formal interrogation, a House member may make a formal request to interrogate the bill or amendment sponsor. If the party opposite agrees, there are still layers of formality that prevent the exchange from becoming caustic.

"Debate has to be addressed to the Speaker," says Myer. He adds that the provision allows members to gain information about the bill in order to make a decision. "You can't use interrogation to do a Perry

Mason type thing," he says.

A transcription of a debate might read as follows:

> Speaker: "The chair recognizes the gentleman from Allegheny County."
>
> Questioner: "Thank you, Mr. Speaker. Mr. Speaker, I rise to question the maker of the amendment."
>
> Speaker: "The maker of the amendment indicates that she agrees to the interrogation."
>
> Questioner: "Mr. Speaker, the maker of the amendment alleges that her legislation would have no impact whatsoever on the Commonwealth's gun manufacturing industry, is this correct?"
>
> Amendment Maker: "That is correct, Mr. Speaker."
>
> Questioner: "Mr. Speaker, how is it then that the National Rifle Association and every major Second Amendment organization calls this, and I quote . . ."
>
> Speaker: "The gentleman from Allegheny County will

suspend. The purpose of interrogation is to provide the maker of the amendment with an opportunity to gain information. This is not the time to debate the issue. Is there a question, or would you prefer to make a statement on the bill?"

Questioner: "Thank you, Mr. Speaker. I withdraw the question and ask that I be permitted to make a statement on the amendment."

Speaker: "The gentleman from Allegheny County is in order and may proceed."

Throughout this exchange, it's entirely possible that the Speaker is cracking the gavel to restore order to the House, pleading for members to provide deference to the members previously recognized. The point of all of this, says Myer, is according maximum deference to elected members. Jealously guarding this right is the job of every Speaker of the House.

In the parliamentary precedents governing legislative activity, the right of a member to be heard is preeminent: "A member once recognized and having the floor is entitled to freedom from interruptions unless something arises that requires immediate consideration" *(Mason's Legislative Manual).*

Through their elected leaders, the people will have a voice. Under this system, the opinions of the people, heard through their elected leaders, will not be impeded.

The point is that passions of the moment, even at their hottest and most emotional, are filtered through the Speaker's rostrum. Like a water filtration system, the Speaker of the House screens out the toxicities that would impede the flow of discussion. While not completely disarmed, verbal bullets maintain sound and fury, but because of the rules are no longer deadly.

The founding generation had witnessed too many seemingly mundane disagreements become wars between men of honor. Duels and fist fights time and again justified the concerns of those who constructed the framework by which we hold public debates to this day.

According to Myer, activity of the House falls under the authority of the Constitution, state statutes, adopted House Rules, and two books: Paul Mason's *Manual of Legislative Procedure* and *A Manual of Legislative Practice* by Thomas Jefferson.

Thomas Jefferson wrote rules, originally published in 1801, that still guide the United States Congress and several legislative bodies like the Pennsylvania House of Representatives. Paul Mason's work from the 1930s is routinely updated to reflect current judicial and legislative precedents.

In Mason's book, the chapter on decorum begins with a rather elegant subhead: "Equality of Members in Debate." It waxes philosophical about "the absolute equality of the members." It's here that the American legislative system is in full bloom:

> It is the duty of all members to conduct themselves so as not to obstruct the rights of other members. Freedom of speech involves obedience to the rules of debate. The language used by members during debate should be temperate, decorous, and respectful. *(Mason's Legislative Manual)*

And if any ambiguity remained, this section of the definitive legislative guidebook, pulled from Jefferson and a handful of other authors, grows even more precise:

> During debate, while the presiding officer is speaking, or the house is engaged in voting, no one is to disturb another in a speech by hissing, coughing, spitting, speaking, or whispering to another, nor passing between the presiding officer and the member speaking, nor crossing the floor of the house, nor walking up and down, nor taking books or papers from the desk, nor writing there. *(Mason's Legislative Manual)*

No matter how much the public's debate slides outside the walls of civil discourse, decorum is designed to preserve a climate where Lincoln's "better angels" might overcome human arrogance and pride.

The responsibility for maintaining that ideal temperature in state legislatures falls to Clancy Myer and 49 other parliamentarians.

MASTER OF DEBATE: BRETT O'DONNELL

At Liberty University, my academic career was a haphazard zigzag around required math courses and other inconvenient obstacles. Between taking semesters off for adventures like interning for the hard-charging freshman senator from Pennsylvania, Rick Santorum, I'd sign up for classes that sounded potentially interesting. In Dr. Brett O'Donnell's class on presidential elections, I found someone who understood that politics was the story of great ideas inhabiting much smaller, and always flawed, men and women.

In addition to teaching, O'Donnell was a rising star on the collegiate debate circuit, leading Liberty to a string of consecutive national titles against names like Harvard, Dartmouth, and Michigan. As the university struggled to gain national credibility in football and basketball, the debate team was on fire, and O'Donnell was invited to *The Colbert Report* to explain their noteworthy success.

The Republican political world took notice immediately, and O'Donnell became the message guru for several national candidates who were challenged with making a human connection in larger audiences. Both George W. Bush and John McCain enlisted him for debate preparations. Mitt Romney's Florida primary turnaround was the result of O'Donnell's messaging intervention.

Today, O'Donnell's behind-the-curtain advice to GOP senators, members of Congress, and governors cuts through swaths of red-state America, along with some notable blue spots. When I connected with him in the weeks before the November 2016 election, he'd just returned with triumphant tales as homestretch advisor to Brexit's surprise superstar, Boris Johnson. O'Donnell's ability to focus even the wildest public personalities is a skill that requires an innate understanding of human nature. Even politicians, who carry the burdens and insecurities of celebrity, respond to brutal honesty—especially when their careers hang in the balance. O'Donnell understands that the message is the candidate. Disconnecting the two is disastrous.

AMERICAN DEBATE: ROOTED IN RESPECT & EQUALITY

Unlike legislative debate, decorum required for political campaigns is relatively subjective. Campaign styles swing between formal and casual, with the pendulum getting stuck lately in the casual position due to social media. On Facebook and Twitter, there is no forced deference or required niceties from Jefferson's handy rulebook to buffer the blows of an opponent's attacks.

DECORUM

"There are no rules. There have been norms, and they have been accepted in terms of how you engage another candidate," says O'Donnell. The origin of the modern, issue-based debate is far more recent than America's founding. "The norms that we have reach all the way back to the Lincoln-Douglas Debates," he said. "Those were really the first memorable set of issue-oriented debates that we know a lot about."

Neither participant in the seven long-form debates of 1858 would understand the spectacle of the WWE-style multi-candidate brawls of 2016. For over one hundred and fifty years, America's politics kept returning to the standard they established that year. Today, the policy-centric debate format has nearly disappeared.

O'Donnell explained that American debate is unique among modern democracies. For example, while Americans expect at least the pretense of substance, the Brits tolerate public debate that's decidedly more caustic and confrontational. However low campaigns fall on the messaging of TV ads and attack mailers, at least the big-stage American politicians have typically maintained a pretense of seriousness.

O'Donnell recalled the moment during the 2012 primary debate season when Minnesota Governor Tim Pawlenty balked at repeating the hybrid phrase he'd been using on the trail to describe Mitt Romney's healthcare reforms in Massachusetts. His inability to repeat the word "Obamneycare" when sharing the stage with Romney displayed a tension between old-world deference and an emerging norm that holds no punches. His public quandary foretold a rapid exit from the field.

In the 2016 debates between Donald Trump and Hillary Clinton, even Trump seemed to understand the presence of the great invisible line separating offstage and onstage decorum. At the conclusion of one of these imbroglios, Trump famously told reporters in the spin room that he'd held back a public shaming of Mrs. Clinton's husband, former President Bill Clinton. The self-restraint wouldn't stick in the next debate when Trump invited several of Clinton's female accusers to sit in the audience, within camera range. Trump's initial hesitation seemed to signal that he knew the precise moment he crossed the line. Without a revival of public manners, it's unlikely he will be the only one.

AMERICAN PUBLIC DISCOURSE: GLADIATORS OR STATESMEN?

O'Donnell's points on the gulf separating American public discourse from the British version is an interesting visual. The U.S. House of Representatives experiences its share of interruptions during legislative business, including a recent post-session congressional sit-in for C-SPAN cameras. An empty House chamber for one-minute member speeches is the other vehicle for more impassioned rhetoric.

In contrast, Prime Minister's Questions, the spirited thrust and parry between the British PM and her opposing interrogators, is nothing like the American experience. In PMQs, the opposition leader and rank-and-file MPs from the opposition bench lob verbal grenades across the narrow divide separating the two sides. The culture of the exchange allows for a cacophony of howls, jeers, and laughter that test the composure of every Prime Minister.

The British system, according to O'Donnell, came from the notion of a nation ruled at a gladiator's roundtable, with the landowning nobility charting policy. In a system led by the royal and titled, there was no guaranteed equality.

"Not only is British public discourse rooted in the roundtable with gladiators, but there was also a very definitive notion of class," he argues. "Theirs was a battle-oriented rhetoric."

The American ideal, reflected in the *Declaration of Independence* and woven into the intellectual writings of the founding generation, was styled in a dramatically different way. Natural rights and human equality have, in each successive generation, been improved, extending the invitation to disenfranchised members of American society, from women to African-Americans. "The notion of equality of discourse got us to the norms we have. America's discourse is a 'value-laden discourse,'" argues O'Donnell. "Everyone is made in the image of God. We all have rights."

BEYOND 2016: REDISCOVERING EQUALITY

When the varying histories of the Trump-Clinton election are finally submitted, one question will remain unanswered for at least a generation: did the savage nature of this period of American public discourse, and the abandonment of the standards of decorum, signal an end to this piece of our experiment in civility?

Beyond the big question, we'll see whether this year was an anomaly or the beginning of an altogether new course for American debate. With an increasingly agnostic view toward the religious faith that shaped the American ideals of human dignity and equality, how do we find our way again? If we decide that we've traveled too far outside the ethical and moral lines drawn from religious tradition, how do we recover?

Answering these questions is up to us.

DECORUM

Decorum recognizes that humans are weighed down by imperfections. The rules of discourse are necessary to protect us from ourselves.

Decorum acknowledges that public debate between opposing and imperfect combatants demands a buffer only institutional rules can provide.

Decorum elevates the public discourse to the level of ideas by placing measures above the flaws of mere men and women.

Decorum encompasses the rules of engagement that grant every participant an equal voice in the public square.

Hon. Chad Mayes, Photographer: Joel Coleman

Hon. Dave Reed, Photographer: Bill Crawford

"Senator Smith has now talked for 23 hours and 16 minutes. It is the most unusual and spectacular thing in the Senate annals. One lone and simple American, holding the greatest floor in the land. What he lacked in experience, he's made up in fight. But those tired Boy Ranger legs are buckling, bleary eyed, voice gone, he cannot go on much longer. And all official Washington is here to be in on the kill."

H.V. KALTENBORN, CBS RADIO
in *Mr. Smith Goes to Washington*

CHAPTER THREE

IDEALISM

Hon. Chad Mayes, California State Assembly, Minority Leader
Hon. Dave Reed, Pennsylvania General Assembly, Majority Leader

I recently met one of the resident preservationists responsible for the ongoing, multi-year restoration of the 1912 Pennsylvania State Capitol. I asked him about one of my favorite spots in the building, the Majority Leader's suite. As the former treasury room, the original space, a full hallway's length in size, was designed like a Main Street bank lobby. Over the years, the grandeur of the room fell victim to repurposing.

In our short exchange in line at Harrisburg's Yellow Bird Café, the restoration expert shared how, in the process of removing suspended ceilings and other remodeling oddities, his team could smell decades of caked-on cigarette smoke. The Leader's office was a dealmaker's den.

Pennsylvania's incomparable Capitol is a museum of the noble and ignoble deeds of its leaders, and smoke-filled rooms are a big part of the mystique. Long before the introduction of the first bill, construction of the people's palace was scandalized by budget overruns and corruption.

When coal was king and lobbyists for the Pennsylvania Railroad roamed legislative chambers and offices, the Keystone State extended hospitality to the kind of cigar-chomping bosses Frank Capra immortalized in the film *Mr. Smith Goes to Washington*. The caricatures of Capra's pre-War political classic aren't far from the descriptions of Pennsylvania's days as a frenzied political trading post. The manufacturing mecca boasted a capitol building reflecting its rising economic influence and national prominence.

President Theodore Roosevelt dedicated the current structure in October of 1906, opening with a few lines of Pennsylvania history before firing off a litany of warnings about the legislature's responsibility to right the abuses of industrial blessings. The speech was no ribbon-cutting pablum. "But each generation has its special and serious difficulties—and we of this generation have to struggle with evils springing from the very material success of which we are so proud, from the very growth and prosperity of which, with justice, we boast," Roosevelt bellowed. "The extraordinary industrial changes of the last half-century have produced a totally new set of conditions, under which new evils flourish, and for these new evils new remedies must be devised."

The president was a gifted retail politician, but he was also a lifelong student of the human heart and its seemingly endless seductions. From his temporary pulpit, the righteous crusader cautioned that if unchecked, Pennsylvania's glimmering new temple could become a house of ill repute:

> (N)ever before have the opportunities for selfishness been so great, nor the results of selfishness so appalling; for in communities where everything is organized on a merely selfish commercial basis, such selfishness, if unchecked, may transform the great forces of the new epoch into powers of destruction hitherto unequaled.

Roosevelt's pastoral chiding would do little to prune the Commonwealth's budding culture of institutional corruption. Pennsylvania's size and relative wealth would guarantee that good government would always be susceptible to viruses.

In spite of these ignoble challenges, genuine public servants still volunteered to run for office. In the years after World War I and World War II, veterans would enter the public's service trained for conditions far more threatening than party war rooms. They brought an ability to overlook ideological, ethnic, and economic differences for the common cause. Ironically these are the same differences that keep today's legislators divided into uncooperative, tribal cells. War was a unifying event long after its conclusion.

IDEALISM

But even Eagle Scouts and decorated war veterans cannot permanently hold back the wildfires of corruption. Eventually, the appetite for power overtakes the noblest motives. Following every period of government reform, the ghosts of Roosevelt's warnings would spark to life.

Well into the early 2000s, many legislators were still deeply grafted into the network of patronage-dispensing privilege. Prizes like entry-level PennDOT positions and the gifting of departmental "ghost jobs" to friends was still part of the portfolio for many senior members. The experienced bulls populating the ranks of chairmanships and leadership positions were often quite generous with government largess.

When I was first elected, controversial WAMs (Walk Around Money) gave each of us a modest allotment to issue grants for local charities and fire departments. With the more controversial votes, legislative leaders could dramatically expand the size of state grant money for pet projects. Some lawmakers would withhold votes from governors and leaders until the last possible moment, waiting for the highest possible payout.

The results of these practices were more complicated. Voters didn't automatically revolt against gift-bearing legislators. In fact, citizens in a pre-Tea Party world expected lawmakers to bring home their pound of budget bacon.

Pennsylvania congressmen like Johnstown's Jack Murtha and

Everett's Bud Shuster procured millions in funding for everything from roads and bridges to treatment programs and prisons. Their floor trading skills returned some measure of dignity to areas shamed by staggering unemployment and the dark, precipitous decline of big industry. With hospitals and courthouses as the last major employment center in many rural counties, congressional largess was like gifting a new suit to a homeless man—dressed for success with nowhere to go.

Local leaders of Pennsylvania's rural and industrial communities understood that in order to save their fading communities, they had to work the system that existed. Voters expected candidates for office to sing the hymns of reform while working within the confines of a less virtuous system.

LAST IN LINE: JOHN PERZEL AND BILL DEWEESE

On Swearing-in Day of January 2001, the Pennsylvania House chamber was decorated like a wedding chapel stuffed with a few hundred floral arrangements. It was the first day I would hear and see the opposing caucus leaders argue from their podiums in the well, set below either side of the Speaker's rostrum.

Majority Leader John Perzel, from Philadelphia, was a former maître d' who ran the Republican caucus like his old restaurant,

IDEALISM

intent on delivering even the smallest request or accommodation to loyal patrons. The power structure he devised was built on thousands of mostly unseen deliveries, from an extra cell phone for a House member, to granting staff healthcare benefits or enlarging the furniture budget.

When it came time to count votes for tax hikes, legislative pay increases, or the takeover of the patronage-laden Philadelphia Parking Authority, Perzel's hat was an endless source of rabbits. When collecting votes from small-government conservatives, his most useful tool was reminding legislators of the catalog of grant requests delivered to his office under their signatures.

With the experience of handling some of Philly's most difficult restaurant patrons, Perzel instinctually sensed when a member of his caucus was weakening. In his old profession, a potential embarrassment could be headed off with a better table or bottle of wine. While not given to mesmerizing floor speeches, his personal charm, resourcefulness, and creativity were rarely outclassed.

Although I can't recall the substance of Perzel's remarks on my first Swearing-in Day, I do remember that he and his team were already busy filling the requests of every member in our freshman class. A speech was a flourish and formality; the real work happened behind the curtain.

Minority Leader Bill DeWeese was Perzel's opposite in nearly every way. While Perzel was introverted, DeWeese was glad-handing and gregarious. While Perzel's vocabulary was unadorned and efficient, DeWeese took every chance to flood sentences with his latest etymological discovery. Listening to him was pure fun.

Perzel was the political lumberjack, felling entire forests with the patient, consistent motions of an ax. DeWeese was a showman, pulling every eye and ear from his first second at the microphone. Perzel wore the plain uniform of a Union League Republican; DeWeese would parade onto the House floor in a seersucker suit, white bucks, bowtie, and Rolex. No one enjoyed the pageantry of public office more than Bill DeWeese.

These two men dominated much of the building's perpetual gossip. They were larger than life, and in Perzel's case, wielded a massive amount of personal and constitutional power.

Witnessing Bill DeWeese and John Perzel from the rank-and-file was like watching two barkers compete for customers at dueling carnival tents. They were the last of a long line of old-school leaders who prized loyalty above almost any other virtue.

Bill DeWeese filled his tent by using the natural gifts of storytelling, self-deprecation, and genuine friendship. He knew the name and life story of every waitress and reporter who crossed his path.

John Perzel rarely made eye contact, but his senses were alert to the slightest move to undercut his widening orbit of authority. Ever the introvert, he was kind and generous to his wife and inner circle but powered through Capitol hallways with a single-mindedness that left no room for small talk. On the job, Perzel was all business.

When both men went to jail during the ascent of an ambitious Attorney General, each responded to the political debasement and public shaming in different ways. Perzel drew inward, communicated with a handful of friends, and read biographies. DeWeese sized up his medium security environs and built a web of friendships from the mess hall to the guard shack of a remote, rural prison ironically named "Retreat Correctional Facility."

By the time each quietly returned for post-prison prospecting visits to the Capitol, both men found that the building had begun to promote a different type of leader. Instead of charmers and dealmakers, the parties turned to management types and policy wonks. In Washington and Harrisburg, lawmakers and their constituents wanted less personality and more business skill.

LEADING THROUGH AN AGE OF INCIVILITY: CHAD MAYES AND DAVE REED

As I'm writing this, Republican Assemblyman Chad Mayes and Republican Representative Dave Reed have never met. While I've known both personally for nearly 20 years, there's no reason either would have been in the same room until now, as each holds the post of Leader in their respective legislative caucus.

In the tiny nest that comprises state legislative leaders, the two represent a pivot toward these changing leadership criteria. It's a profile almost unrecognizable to the cajoling backslappers of the previous era. Mayes, aged 39, is the Minority Leader in the California State Assembly. Reed, aged 38, is the Majority Leader in the Pennsylvania House of Representatives.

The contrast in their state leadership roles is the same stylistic separation between current House Speaker Paul Ryan and his Reagan-era predecessor, Tip O'Neill. In personal temperament and style, Mayes and Reed manage and encourage, using few carrots or sticks to achieve unity. Finding consensus based on rational, fact-based argument is the new way.

Despite many similarities, Harrisburg and Sacramento are worlds apart. As the Assembly's Minority Leader, Mayes presides over a caucus in Sacramento whose relevance to the process is almost non-existent. Demographic shifts and the absence of a widely known and respected statewide Republican leader deepen the Golden State's blue status with each passing year.

In the near future, Mayes could become a major part of his party's solution. The *Los Angeles Times* recently speculated that Mayes might be the only political figure able to reverse the GOP's downward tumble in California. In the same month, other news stories suggested that Reed deserves a similarly prominent leadership role in the next chapter of Pennsylvania's GOP.

While I miss the characters that inhabited the old political world, what we've lost in the thrilling unpredictability of their personalities we've gained in the steady, unemotional leadership represented by this new generation. This was a much-needed change.

When I sat down separately with Mayes and Reed in the days before November's election, I wanted to understand the way in which they approached leading members in this year's toxic political environment. Without knowing how the top of the ticket would inflate or deflate their prospects, both men had the unenviable assignment of defending and winning legislative seats.

IDENTITY BEYOND PARTY

As long as I've known both men, each has wrestled with the idea of casually suiting up for partisan cheerleading. The Republican label is sometimes too narrow—and often too broad—to explain what either man believes. For each, blind partisanship is a thoughtless alternative to the exercise of solving complex policy issues.

Being Republican has never been either's first identity. The priorities of faith, marriage, and parenthood have deepened their reluctance to be defined by politics. Even within the Republican walls of his legislative district, Reed campaigns on a "People before Politics" slogan, and routinely wins an outsized percentage of Democratic votes.

"I'm policy oriented," says Reed. "If Governor Wolf wants to work on a policy item I think is good, I'll work with him." Even with a nearly unstoppable Republican majority, he still believes in coalitions: "You've got to find your dance partner on any particular issue, and it shouldn't matter if they're Republican or Democrat."

Both Reed and Mayes hold to conservative, Republican orthodoxy on most issues, but neither wants to miss the chance to understand the other side. While neither has changed many of their philosophical views since accepting their statewide leadership posts, the delivery of their messages is tempered by the need to advance policies.

Like national Republicans, both men are traditionalists on social and family policies but are reluctant to exploit sincerely held differences with opponents to fundraise or target the opposition. Both view public policy as a set of challenges to be resolved with careful planning, coalition building, and tactical execution. Unlike a generation of pollsters and consultants, neither sees ideas as voter bait designed to draw out the opposing passions of hope or fear.

For Dave Reed, preparation for legislative battles includes a technique of reverse prosecution. "The first thing I try to do is formulate in my mind what case I would make if I were arguing the exact opposite position." Reed knows that patient listening is key to depersonalizing political issues. "I think if you can understand their arguments—even if you disagree with them—it helps you keep focused on the policy, not the personalities," he says. "Most people—even if they're

IDEALISM

in opposition to you—are not bad people."

As lawmakers representing districts more partisan and philosophically conservative than large sections of their respective states, both men are susceptible to charges that their leadership style lacks the firebrand qualities many demand. As caucus leaders, each is required to balance the requests of both conservative and progressive members while advancing their larger agendas.

When pressed, Mayes frequently turns to basic civics. "In a democracy, the legislature is reflective of its people," he says. In California, even the most committed conservatives must choose between the role of policy persuader or rhetorician.

As the Republican Leader, he often hears his constituents saying, "you just need to blow that place up." His response is, "Okay, after it's blown up, then what? The truth is that it gets rebuilt in exactly the same way."

Unlike the pivotal scene in *Mr. Smith Goes to Washington*, when Jimmy Stewart's character, Senator Jefferson Smith, sweats it out during the famous filibuster scene, waiting for any word of public support, opinions in today's legislatures pour into every minute of a politician's consciousness. Facebook opinion often beats the speed and accuracy of traditional polling data. While a politician may not always be responsive, trends on the ground are no longer difficult to divine.

As young politicians in highly visible roles, Reed and Mayes are even less insulated from the temperamental swings of the public mood. Technology has popped the isolating bubble that once allowed politicians to control the pace of conversation. Today, voters are in charge, and both Mayes and Reed understand this better than many of their more seasoned peers.

For Reed, technology can dilute the authenticity and necessary grit of a real conversation. He offsets the thousands of virtual connections with a tradition of perpetually knocking on doors and holding town hall meetings. Beyond measuring the response of posts and tweets, in-person contact is always the best way to check the public's pulse.

During a recent public session in one of the southernmost parts of his sprawling rural district, Reed fielded a question about a rumored plan by President Obama to ban the Pledge of Allegiance. Had he heard about it? What was his view? Reed replied that he hadn't seen or heard anything about it, but expected he would have if it were legitimate. The story was proven false; there was no plan to ban the Pledge.

Chad Mayes believes the motivation behind online gossip may be more sinister. Behind every unchecked rumor could exist a cash-hungry political fundraising entity. "There's always a fight going on," he says. "The way they get people motivated is to create some level of fear or excitement. Their real goal is to keep their organization afloat."

Facebook and Twitter serve as tools for personal connection and the promise of neighborhood and community. In the hands of a political or fundraising consultant, they serve as easy platforms for fear-based manipulation. "What we've created across this country is the ability to monetize democracy," says Mayes.

For now, both men have decided that respectful responses to every rumor or unchecked story are best. Rebuilding a culture of civility in politics is partly their responsibility, with politicians and constituents still learning how to apply traditional standards of decorum to virtual conversation.

"Things that folks wouldn't sit down and write in a letter or come into your office and say, they say in social media," says Reed. Controlling his response begins by remembering that "his opponents are human beings."

This year, Reed's personal kindness and candor won him a political stew of endorsements from labor giant AFL-CIO as well as near ideological opposites like the Pennsylvania Pro-Life Federation, the Pennsylvania Chamber of Business and Industry, and the National Rifle Association. He prizes principled independence.

"When I leave this position, I want folks to look at me and say, 'you could not pigeonhole him or buy him in any way,'" he says. This is the way in which he prevents the political process from destroying idealism. With eyes wide open, Dave Reed still believes in public service.

Like Reed, Mayes prizes civility and has built deep friendships across the political and ideological spectrum that have helped emotionally charged debates between evangelical Christians and the

LGBTQ community graduate to civil, respectful discussions.

In December, the *Los Angeles Times* praised Mayes for playing clean and winning fair. The article noted the fact that Mayes has never run negative ads against any of his political opponents, saying, "He turns the other cheek if attacked, and not just during the Christmas season." The article continued, "One thing the Yucca Valley legislator definitely is not is a Donald Trump Republican. Mayes is civil and respectful. He doesn't call people liars or crooks or losers."

Both Reed and Mayes prove that true civility doesn't always require surrender or capitulation.

LIFE BEYOND POLITICS AND 2016

When I asked each of them about the potential aftershocks of the 2016 election, neither seemed too worried that the lawless tone of public discourse would forever replace America's tradition of civility. In their view, this year's election was out of sync with the character of public debates rooted in the ideals of equality and good faith.

Chad Mayes talked at some length about his awareness that the position and the accompanying notoriety were temporary gifts. "At the end of all this, people are going to forget who I am," he said. His advice to aspiring leaders is blunt: "If you're thinking about becoming involved in public service, your goal should be a cause bigger than yourself."

For Dave Reed, the year's bitterness requires a broader view. "There's a plan," he says, "and it's not ours. I have faith that God will take care of it. He will provide."

In a widely shared op-ed in *The Desert Sun*, Mayes penned his conclusion to the matter:

> Hallelujah! The 2016 election is over, and we can finally all breathe a sigh of relief. Honestly, I can't remember an election season as dark and divisive as the one we just experienced. The mean-spirited and fear-mongering tactics used by both parties brought out the worst in all of us.
>
> I have spent the last several months pondering why so many people act like bad-mannered children in American politics. Running for office doesn't have to be a blood sport. We can and should be civil, intelligent, and honorable in our campaigning.
>
> If we are honest with ourselves, both Republicans and Democrats have serious problems, and much healing needs to take place within our nation.

Will Dave Reed's and Chad Mayes' idealism fade as they enter their forties and confront the strength and endurance of old politics? Or do they represent the beginning of a hope-filled return to a public service and civic engagement not anchored in cynicism and fear? So far, they've chosen the latter and succeeded.

IDEALISM

Idealism uses the mechanism of a political party without being controlled by it.

Idealism says that when political loyalties cross conviction and conscience, conscience is the only choice.

Idealism sees past the excuses and failures of old methods to imagine principled answers to lingering problems.

Idealism maintains optimism rooted in an eternal, unchanging source of hope.

Dan Rather, Photographer: Lynne Goldstein

Scott Detrow, Photographer: Joel Coleman

"If you look for truth, you may find comfort in the end; if you look for comfort you will not get either comfort or truth only soft soap and wishful thinking to begin, and in the end, despair."

C.S. LEWIS

CHAPTER FOUR

TRUTH

Dan Rather, Reporter, former anchor, CBS Evening News
Scott Detrow, NPR Political Reporter

I used to love talk radio. As a conservative-minded teenager, I loved every second of Rush Limbaugh. He launched proverbial cannon balls into the high fort of liberalism and progressive thinking, and it was thrilling. With Rush, you never needed original sources or the polluted filtration of the mainstream media.

With the snap and rustle of paper held in "formerly nicotine-stained hands," Limbaugh introduced his audience to the giants of conservative thought without requiring us to labor through books or white papers. Limbaugh invited us to meet the thinkers of the *Wall Street Journal* editorial page and hear from institutional, conservative vanguards like *Human Events*, *National Review*, and the Heritage Foundation.

It was Rush who taught us the difference between a Rockefeller Republican and the Reagan, Kemp, and Buckley kind.

Ironically, it was also Rush who helped us find the narrow path to support establishment nominees like George H.W. Bush and Bob Dole when favorites like Pat Buchanan faltered. He taught young conservatives how to fight.

The idea of Rush mocked the clubhouse conservatives who never got dirty. Their ideas never left the debating society. They pondered and lectured, but to them it was all theory. Rush sent a producer with a microphone into the streets of Manhattan to poke at the culture of entitlement and elitism. His animal rights updates skewered the humanization of pets and the blindness of those who refused to recognize their dehumanizing view of unborn human life. He took the battle outside the walls of think tanks, and millions of his self-proclaimed Dittoheads cheered.

The pointy-headed intellectuals holed up in ivory towers never sang our song, but he did. His original, guestless, three-hour marathon was and remains the show prep for every other AM talk-radio mimic. His dominance of the revitalized medium saved hundreds of fading stations from extinction and eventually created demand for conservative bloggers and alternative news sources.

When Rush parodied trendy, feelings-heavy cause ribbons with dollar bills folded into "budget deficit awareness" ribbons, I dutifully pinned mine. I spent my allowance on his books and bumper stickers.

I loved everything represented by the on-air insurgency Rush delivered fifteen hours a week. The man behind the Golden EIB

Microphone was taking on the networks, the establishment, and often the Congress and the White House.

A few decades later, I've all but sworn-off Rush and his fellow AM talkers. It's less of a breakup and more of a slow migration away from pre-processed thinking. Forming views with integrity has required a replacement of entertainment politics with independent reading and revised study habits. While I'll always be grateful that Rush heightened my curiosity for news, I'm disappointed that I didn't learn to be a discerning consumer earlier in life.

But I'm not the only one who suffered from a daily intake of light news. There's an entire generation making decisions on weighty, consequential events within seconds, not minutes, of receiving information.

Because of the shorter attention spans and narrowing interests of audiences, talk radio and cable news are now yielding to quick skims and tabloid-style apps as the primary purveyors of journalistic content. The customized experience reduces stories and headlines to their most provocative minimums, and each repackaged story is laced with heavy doses of satire and sarcasm to keep audiences stocked for online debates.

TRUTH

TRUTH CHECKERS, NOT NEWS SOURCES

I'm not at all suggesting that consumable news bytes aren't useful ways to wedge otherwise ignored content into an already-overloaded brain space. The snack-friendly news keeps us from embarrassing ourselves if we're stopped by a *Tonight Show* reporter or chosen for *Jeopardy*! But if our Instagram and Twitter feeds are our primary sources of information, we're in serious trouble.

Things get especially dicey when we're retweeting memes on Planned Parenthood, the Israeli-Palestinian conflict, Vladimir Putin's election shenanigans, and the Chinese island construction in the South China Sea. Some issues won't squeeze into the space of a tweet.

At best, talk shows and bloggers hold the mainstream media accountable for missing or ignoring essential pieces of a story. Opinionated crowdsourcing delivers an important, and often unrecognized, public service. Every journalist has a philosophical or professional blindspot, and despite intentions to be fair and balanced, coverage is never a perfect blend of either.

Indeed, a host like Rush does not approach events in search of new facts. He's not a journalist, and he doesn't pretend to hide biases. He scans stories for facts that enhance a cartooned interpretation of the story he's constructing.

With entertainment-driven programming, each host stays within the script. In 2016, Sean Hannity began promoting the Trump candidacy. The former Rush Limbaugh fill-in welcomed opponents on his programs, but only as supporting cast and in a way that prevented any serious undermining of the candidate. Notably, when Senator Ted Cruz avoided "endorsing" Trump on the Convention stage, Hannity's generosity toward the reality TV star ended.

Amidst the slow death of independent, investigative newspaper reporting, citizens are more vulnerable than ever to lies and demagogues. Neutralizing the power of a free and independent press, and thus limiting their ability to hold politicians and government agencies accountable, isn't the prescription for eradicating media bias. The Fourth Estate must survive for the other three branches of democracy to thrive.

BEFORE RUSH, DAN RATHER

Many of us who live on the center-right side of the philosophical spectrum at first cheered the demise of old media institutions like CBS News. Staff cuts at the *New York Times* or trouble at *Newsweek* appeared to be the logical result of news organizations failing to adapt. The mainstream media didn't get us, and we didn't need their slanted interpretations. Good riddance.

A prime example of this seemed to be the exit of Dan Rather as the last king of the MSM (Mainstream Media). Perhaps the best way to describe Rather's relationship with many conservatives is to compare it with my late Filipino grandfather's relationship with anyone of Japanese origin. While too young to enlist in the Filipino resistance movement, my late grandfather allegedly became a runner for the American forces and Filipino Scouts. Undoubtedly, he witnessed or heard first-hand accounts of the invading army's daily atrocities. He never forgave them.

We conservatives have always had our own rogues' gallery of enemy generals and lieutenants, and it has always included the anchors of primetime network news. Perhaps our views were formed during the Nixon years when his enemy list always included journalists. Dan Rather himself was on Nixon's radar, and conservatives never took their eyes off him.

But is the caricature of the media justified? Did their ideological tilt create the opening for alternative outlets? After all, reporters always tossed the embarrassing, lowbrow questions to conservatives—for example, when Katie Couric broadsided Sarah Palin about her daily reading list.

The theory of bias is then confirmed when Mike Huckabee receives the lone question about evolution, and Rick Santorum is the designated receiver for all things LGBTQ. To conservatives, the media narrative positioned liberal candidates as personally flawed but intellectually curious and sincerely motivated. Conservatives, on the other hand, were intellectually limited, hypocritical, and given to prehistoric fears about God's judgment.

It is the cumulative list of events and experiences that forms the charge of "liberal bias."

For Evangelicals, traditional Catholics, and conservative Jews, the problem seemed even more pronounced. According to the media, those with deeply held religious beliefs were too often spilling over into public decision-making and violating the rules of a pluralistic, post-religious society. Examples abound, like the time when presidential candidate George W. Bush cited Jesus Christ as his hero during a candidate forum and was greeted by sneering reporters, adding fuel to the perception that he lacked "gravitas."

In the world of perception, headline writers and assignment editors seemed to penalize any politicians who believed in or, worse yet, lived by their religious values.

When conservatives listen to the news, we pick up on every nuance of snide condescension. Already sensitive to slights, we expect every nightly newscast to sound something like this:

> In other news, Republican Senator Tom Johnson, a longtime opponent of women's reproductive rights and fierce critic of public education, will enter the race for governor this Tuesday. Johnson is a four-time state senator and longtime opponent of climate change science and commonsense gun regulations. The White House recently expressed dismay at

> his support for what they called "debunked religious theories about human origins." Johnson supports so-called "intelligent design" theories, which experts call a re-branded form of Creationism. Most polls place Mr. Johnson within five points of the incumbent, but observers don't expect the race to be competitive as more of his controversial views emerge. We'll be providing live coverage and fact-checking of the Johnson announcement this Monday.

Dan Rather, who had the unfortunate timing of assuming the anchor chair at the beginning of Ronald Reagan's conservative rise and inheriting the most trusted news program, would always be conservative's media enemy #1.

"Rather biased" bumper stickers were a conservative favorite, and his unwillingness to stop acting as a reporter when he took Walter Cronkite's place made him the perfect foil. Rather wasn't just going to be a newsreader.

Most well-known public figures like Dan Rather are remembered in three or four snapshots, images of events dropped into the public consciousness. For Rather, those moments of renown included his famous repartee with President Nixon during a televised press conference before a national convention of broadcasters. When Rather stood to ask the president his question, a divided audience booed and cheered, prompting Nixon to ask, "Are you running for something?"

After the laughter subsided, Rather retorted, "No sir, Mr. President. Are you?"

My first memory of Dan Rather was watching the now-pivotal interview he conducted with Vice President George H.W. Bush. During a hot, televised exchange before the 1988 presidential election, Bush did something of a Trump-style media takedown, expressing outrage at the line of questioning and accusing the anchorman of an on-air ambush. The Bush campaign turned the legitimate line of questioning on the Iran-Contra affair into a liability for CBS at the precise time when the candidate, a decorated World War II aviator, needed some pre-primary toughening. It worked, and the Bush campaign expertly surfed the conflict.

When I watched the 28-year-old clip again on YouTube, I saw things that hadn't been preserved in the lore of the Bush-Rather showdown. Rather was the prepared and focused interrogator. When posing questions on his primary topic, the Iran-Contra Affair, he remained professional and on-point, but deferential to the office and the man. I saw none of the bullying and browbeating recorded in three decades of editorializing. Rather was doing his job as a reporter. The Republican spin worked, but it was untrue.

Of course, it was the famous Rather-led investigation of the second candidate Bush and his confusing National Guard service record that would lead to a forced separation with CBS News.

In his 2012 memoir of his years at CBS News, *Rather Outspo-*

ken, he patiently walks readers through his version of the facts, while carefully avoiding vindictiveness. There's little of the expected score-settling often found in the memoir of someone whose last national moment was overshadowed by controversy. Instead, Rather's book is a reporter's lament on the death of independent journalism and the rise of sensational journalism.

Reading the facts that Rather presents and the subsequent report by the CBS-hired Thornburgh Commission, it's plain that once again, remembrances of this moment deserve serious reconsideration. For anyone interesting in understanding the way in which careers and reputations are drained of truth and repacked into simplistic, partisan narratives, Rather's book is worth a read.

MEETING DAN RATHER

I interviewed Dan Rather less than two weeks before his 85th birthday, as part of a larger project on behalf of the American Middle East Institute (AMEI) in Pittsburgh. AMEI hosts an annual convention to promote stronger business ties between American and Middle Eastern companies, and Rather was their headliner.

Included in my annual AMEI duties is a short interview with the keynote speaker for posterity and the production of a highlights reel of the event. More than anything else, AMEI's confabs provide a framework by which to continue important conversations about ways to strengthen free markets during turbulent times. As Institute founder Simin Curtis often says, even when the Middle East looks darkest, "business marches on."

When I greeted Rather at the door of Carnegie Music Hall, the anchorman looked every bit the part, with a dark suit, trademark suspenders and a long reporter's notebook tucked into his hip pocket. Throughout the night, it became apparent that the latter wasn't a prop. Along with his smartphone, his pen and notebook were essential tools.

From the moment he stepped out of the car to his exit from the backstage loading dock four hours later, he exuded gratitude, making eye contact with the entire crew and letting them know how much he appreciated their service. He defied every stereotype of the media elite. Dan Rather was no prima donna.

RATHER ON THE "CIVILITY OF TONE"

Sitting down in a room that was once purportedly Andrew Carnegie's private study, I wanted to know if the conservative cartoon version of Dan Rather would appear. Was he the media villain who relentlessly tried to dethrone Republican presidents with half-truths and bias? Was he the tragic hero, the fall guy for CBS portrayed by Robert Redford in *Truth*, the 2015 movie about the Bush National Guard story?

By the end of the evening, after watching him give two speeches and patiently pose for hundreds of pictures, I realized the conservatives did not have Dan Rather pegged. In fact, it was apparent that the real Dan Rather was a casualty of the conservative party's objective: to win elections. We got this one wrong.

The presidential election was just weeks ahead, and many Americans had flagged it as the ugliest moment in modern politics. What did Rather think?

He went straight to one of his heroes, Dr. Martin Luther King Jr., paraphrasing a line from the "I Have a Dream" speech about the content of one's character being the necessary glue of civility. Defining people by groups or political parties bypasses the American ideal of individual equality.

"I consider it [civility] to be the most important thing," said Rather. "The civility of tone perhaps is the way I'd put it—to see people as individuals."

King comes up a lot with Rather. As one of the first reporters to cover the early days of the Civil Rights Movement for a major network, he bonded with the young minister whom he considers a role model, along with Mother Teresa and the Dalai Lama.

But what about this moment in our national life? Is civility dead?

No, civility isn't dead, but individual acts of kindness and cooperation can get lost in the crowd. "Americans are at their best, particularly when it's a one-on-one relationship, or maybe a small group," he says. Communities still work because neighbors accept and treat each other as people. "In larger groups, and particularly when it's institution to institution," says Rather, "this sometimes falls away."

Dan Rather believes in and practices civility. He sees the political tone of 2016 as an instance when the noise drowned out the goodness.

RATHER ON GRATITUDE

Where the real Dan Rather cuts hard into the conservative stereotype created for him is on his view of what makes a life virtuous. As young conservatives, we learned to generally categorize liberals as philandering atheists who secretly loathe America and grit their teeth when saluting the flag.

Five minutes with Rather, and this myth evaporates. Take, for example, his routine for "suiting up" for the nightly newscast.

First, he'd call his wife Jean to "steady" him, and then he'd "say a little prayer." Given his nearly-quarter-century career as the CBS *Evening News* anchor, and a marriage that's lasted almost 60 years, that's a lot of prayer and monogamy as a card-carrying member of the media elite.

Although Rather is a fixture in New York, he's still every bit a Texan and generously dispenses down-home colloquialisms. The solitude of rural America is still his default. I ask him how often he steals away to his cabin retreat. "Almost every weekend," he tells me, although the fishing hasn't been great lately.

But what's most interesting is that despite the rollicking ups and downs of his career, Dan Rather isn't bitter or even wistful. He was happy to rehearse the highlights like Vietnam and the hundreds of visits to the Oval Office, but he lives and works in the present. His life is full, and he is grateful.

"I try every day to be deeper and deeper into gratitude, humility, modesty, and behind that, forgiveness, mercy, and yes, love," he tells me. "And I do find that gratitude is something that's understood the world over. Even if you have not one word of the language of the country that you're in—if you make a habit of making it clear that you appreciate how you've been helped, even some small aid given you, and that gratitude is deep within you, it resonates, and it resonates greatly."

If there's an idea most associated with the career of Dan Rather, it is of course courage—a word he once used at the end of nightly broadcasts and reprised for his final signoff on CBS *Evening News*. The reporter who stalked KKK meetings at the height of their power and stared into the murderous eyes of Saddam Hussein, was unwilling to assign the virtue to himself. "I don't have much courage, but I like the word," he says.

"Right behind courage, I think, is gratitude and humility," he says. Speaking as a satisfied customer he continues: "If you radiate a sense of gratitude, humility, and modesty, you can make your way anyplace in the world."

RATHER LANDS ON PLANET FACEBOOK

The night I interviewed him in mid-October, Dan Rather's Facebook page had just crossed the 400,000 mark. At the close of 2016, he had reached nearly 1 million followers.

When I point out his success, he thanks me for noticing. "I have no illusions. I'm deep into gratitude for what we've been able to accomplish on Facebook, but there are plenty of people who have a lot more followers and a lot more clicks than we do." Halfway through his eightieth decade, he talks about his social media experiment like it's his first day at CBS News: "I've landed not just on a different planet, but a different cosmos, and I'm still trying to find my way."

He knows the difficult climb into broadcast media. "I consider myself very lucky. I started in print journalism, wandered into radio, then into television, and now here in the second decade of the 21st century, here I am trying to make my way in social media."

He was warned by social media strategists to keep it short. "Dan, nothing more than two paragraphs," he recalls. "Nobody will pay any attention to it," they said. He started with two, but kept tinkering with the formula, writing until, in his words, he was "filing" posts of essay length.

His model for Facebook, and I suspect for journalism itself, is a CBS broadcast legend who came to prominence in World War II and retired in the late 1970s. He says, "My goal is to do the kind of work the late, great Eric Sevareid did. He was and remains the best writer ever developed in electronic journalism."

But how would Dan Rather be different from the bomb-throwing, emoticon-driven online subculture?

"I'm not trying to cause controversy," he says. "What I'm trying to do is spark some sunburst of thought." And offering a bit of general advice, he adds, "I want people to be thoughtful." His goal is to fuse news events with decades of perspective. "I like to pull back on what we call in television a 'wide shot.' Let's get some context and perspective into what's happening."

RATHER ON THE "POST-TRUTH ERA"

On a recent Facebook Live event, Rather talked about his new Udemy course on journalism before fielding online audience questions. The first question is the one he's been answering in various forms since November: "Does truth still matter?"

With President Donald Trump's penchant for a fluid, non-literal use of words, do political leaders need to mean what they say? Are words used solely for the purpose of bartering and negotiation? Is truth relative?

Rather answers with this warning: "We're in danger of moving into a post-truth political era—a post-facts political era," he says. "Facts matter. Facts really matter."

But as if to avoid the temptation to be anyone's personal standard, he points out the difference between the end we seek and human fallibility. "I'm a lifetime journalist. I've made a lot of mistakes—some might argue I've made every mistake in the book. But I have a passion for reporting the news, and the creed I've tried to do my professional career by is: be accurate, be fair, pull no punches, play no favorites, and try to report the truth, or as close to the truth as humanly possible."

No, Dan Rather as a person and public figure is not the person we remember from a handful of public missteps or breathtakingly impressive career highs. The truth about the major actors on or near history's main stage is worth pursuing, for the sake of truth itself.

SCOTT DETROW: TAILOR-MADE FOR 2016

Scott Detrow got a big break this year. It wasn't his first, but it's likely to be one of the most significant milestones in the world of journalism. While Dan Rather's renewed stature and season of life allow for in-depth interviews, Detrow's generation is elbowing for space in a marketplace questioning the very need for professional journalists.

When NPR tapped the then-31-year-old to lead election year coverage of political technology and data, the interesting side beat became one the best seats on the bus. To stretch the metaphor, he landed in the boiler room of the Trump's Twitter-powered locomotive at the precise moment when traditional journalism and @realDonaldTrump went head to head.

Until 2016, political success was always connected with an ability to cooperate, manipulate, and sometimes intimidate the media. Encounters with reporters was never risk averse, and giving the interview couldn't guarantee the headline or angle the politician hoped would emerge.

In politics, consultants make early retirement helping candidates and their teams learn to dodge the swinging axes and trapdoors of experienced journalists. In my experience, every interview feels like the hidden parts of your soul are being x-rayed. The impression of a reporter's all-seeing eye must be some combination of intuition and training.

Some of the best reporters I've known, like one of Scott Detrow's State Capitol mentors in Harrisburg, the late Pete DeCoursey, had a way of letting you know that while they may like you personally, they still have to ask the question. It might not be painless, but it comes with the job.

For the politician, the objective is always control. Get far ahead of the story by shaping the facts of the narrative before reporters even ask. Like picking a jury, the political communications team feels out reporters willing to listen, or those who are at least fair or undecided. The more successful the politician, the less control possible—at least this was the world before Donald Trump.

On paper, few people were more prepared for 2016 than Scott Detrow. His father is a longtime radio newsman in one of the country's most competitive markets: New York. His father's run includes two decades at ABC Radio and a later stint at AP Radio News.

For Detrow, early preparation for the profession, from voice inflection to the lifestyle expectations of working weekends and holidays, gave a window into his future. But it was during tag-alongs to election night victory parties and New York rallies where his father's craft became something of an obsession for Detrow.

During his college years at Fordham, Detrow worked for New York public radio station WFUV. "Standing there with these hard-edged New York City TV reporters who were all screaming each other down—I learned how to carve out my space." Working in the media market that made Trump a national tabloid celebrity, Detrow previewed much of its later handling of the billionaire candidate's media vetting. New York was "bipartisan in its bloodlust," he said. "When they smell blood, they pounce, and they aggressively pounce."

Anthony Weiner, Michael Bloomberg, and Rudy Giuliani all went under the same ruthless New York media knife. Sharp elbows, fights for platform space, and overlapping questions shouted from the back of the room were all rehearsals for 2016.

DETROW ON THE MYTH OF A MEDIA MONOLITH

After New York, Detrow followed the public radio path to Harrisburg and later to Sacramento. During this time, he learned the art of sourcing—testing and validating the story behind the story.

As a State Capitol reporter, he recalls being somewhat surprised at the intraparty division between House and Senate leadership. Even someone as objectionable to Republicans as Governor Ed Rendell wasn't enough to unify a powerful opposition. Real reporting would require plenty of after-hours trips to political watering holes and the development of trusted, reliable sources.

Politics is complex, and the stories are never simple. "If you're only following it from a distance, you're going to make rash judgments that aren't fully informed," says Detrow.

When he describes the Capitol experience in Harrisburg, Detrow contrasts his time with the New York press sharks and the California press corps. "The Harrisburg press corps was chummy and collegial," he remembers. There, information in the newsroom was more like the wartime bonding in a foxhole. New reporters are shown the ropes and mentored.

The point, argues Detrow, is that media culture varies. "The monolith idea is wrong because I think it's different from market to market," he says. Even within the NPR newsroom, personal views from religion to politics reflect American diversity.

In some markets like New York, a politician's private life is fair game. From extramarital affairs to fashion and food tastes, nothing escapes the media's attention. By contrast, in Pennsylvania, unless personal indiscretions violate the public trust, most reporters stick to straight coverage, steering clear of tabloid news.

DETROW ON THE CHALLENGE OF COVERING TRUMP: TRUST

For the 2016 primaries, NPR beefed up its political reporting division to cover the burgeoning field of top-tier candidates. With some twenty reporters trained on the field, and the added heft of a city-by-city presence through local public radio stations, NPR had the ability to report deep and wide.

Technology. Demographics. Pop culture. The network's plan to cover the eventual nominee would be ambitious and, if successful, would provide unrivaled analysis for its audience. "This allowed us to do bigger-picture reporting," said Detrow. Accordingly, that meant NPR could plumb depths deeper than a candidate's Twitter feed or manufactured controversies.

In the end, the strategy kept the network out of the crosshairs of either side and gave voters an experience offered by few other news sources during this election cycle. But even this plan was rife with challenges.

NPR's first charge to reporters was simple—cover what the candidates are saying and doing.

With some of the more theatrical comments, Trump supporters would ask, "How can you broadcast Donald Trump insulting people today?" The response according to Detrow was straightforward. "When he said things that were not true, we were going to put it in context. We're going to cover what Trump said and we're going to cover what Clinton said." NPR carefully avoided calling a false or inaccurate statement by Trump a "lie," or calling the candidate a "liar." Instead, they would compare statements to known facts.

Secondly, the coverage was to examine big-picture issues. Practically, this meant that Detrow could spend hours gleaning from Trump's bestselling autobiography and other original source material. "How does what he talks about in *The Art of the Deal* reflect how he campaigns?" Detrow asked himself. Detrow also explored less traditional angles like the philosophical camaraderie between Brexit leader and British MP Nigel Farage and the populist phenomenon in America.

Detrow and other NPR reporters covering Trump had the responsibility to protect the network's reputation to follow the story without forcing pieces to fit a preexisting narrative. "I'm not going to find the most incendiary thing I can find, just to stick it to him. I'm going to pick something very representative," says Detrow. "You find the common thread in each of them that gives you the larger picture."

The third category of coverage was perhaps the defining story of the election—the voters themselves. "This was an identity politics election," said Detrow. In light of this, the network attempted to provide coverage beyond the parachute approach taken by cable networks.

The challenge of covering Donald Trump, like all candidates, is the issue of trust. Without it, even the most elaborate story-gathering strategies fail. If press coverage itself becomes the story, voters begin to choose news sources that might or might not meet the high coverage standards and newsgathering resources of a network like NPR.

"You want to be fair, and you want to be viewed as fair," says Detrow. "If people see you as having a point of view, people see you as having a side—selectively deciding what facts to share. You've lost your role as the place both sides can come to, to get what the facts are to begin with. Delivering a fair report means making sure you're not putting on your horse blinders to ignore the facts that you don't want."

At Trump rallies, the candidate understood this better than anyone else. If the press lost its reputation for fairness and was no longer deemed trustworthy, then the only reliable source was his personal interpretation of events. Everything reported, from crowd size to speeches, was sportingly framed as a dispute with the media.

Where Detrow experienced this tension most was in line at Trump rallies. Interviews with supporters in front of the arena-filled throngs were generally "respectful and thoughtful." The longer conversations allowed for a more representative, less provocative sampling of voices from the candidate's base.

Once inside, Trump would inevitably point to the press platform to unleash a stock tirade against the distortions and lies of the coverage of his campaign and the media's alleged refusal to show massive crowd sizes.

As usual, the story was more complicated. According to Detrow, in some instances, Trump's own press team would ask for a tight, fixed shot on the candidate to avoid showing the glass screens and stands of the teleprompters. Media requests for side risers that would have captured the crowd's size were denied. While leading "show the crowd" chants portrayed tactical showmanship, the real objective was to strip reporters of names and identities. Replacing individual reporters with a single villain—The Media—was a masterful tactic.

Once the rally was underway, Detrow would interact with the people he interviewed just moments before. The personal rapport evaporated. "I stopped being 'Scott the guy I talked to for 20 minutes,' and I suddenly became 'the media,'" Detrow recalls.

In the end, Detrow's personal travels with the Trump campaign, which included long, solitary drives through the Nevada desert and flights aboard the Trump press plane, would take him to nearly a dozen battleground states covering 190 electoral votes.

To the end, no matter how pejorative his profession became to Donald Trump supporters, Detrow's refusal to pick sides was steadfast. His job was to report the news.

"If your starting point is that I'm picking and choosing (news content) to make Donald Trump look as bad as possible, then we have a problem, and we're not able to do what we think our job is, which is to tell people what's happening," Detrow says.

At the end of 2016, Trump's strategy had, at least temporarily, declawed the only institution powerful enough to hold him accountable. Like Rush Limbaugh's campaign to discredit network news, the new president was winning the war against the appointed guardians of truth. At year's end, the *NBC News/Wall Street Journal* poll found that only 16% had "a great deal or quite a bit of confidence" in the nation's news media, while 55% had "no confidence."

The framework of American civility cannot survive without the common language and understanding that a free, independent, and trustworthy media provides.

TRUTH

Truth doesn't change when facts are rearranged.

Truth is the foundation of trust, and without it, everything built above it will eventually destroy what remains.

Truth allows men to sleep soundly, experience everyday joys, and never feel threatened by the hounding panic of a lingering lie.

Truth exposes the places where light and love are most needed.

Senator Rick Santorum, Photographer: Bill Crawford

"Courage is not limited to the battlefield, or the Indianapolis 500, or bravely catching a thief in your house. The real tests of courage are much quieter. They are the inner tests, like remaining faithful when nobody's looking, like enduring pain when the room is empty, like standing alone when you're misunderstood."

CHARLES SWINDOLL

CHAPTER FIVE

COURAGE

*Hon. Rick Santorum, former U.S. Senator
and Presidential Candidate*

My sign said "Fat Cats for Wofford," and I had the full costume and headdress to match. Standing outside the opponent's fundraiser was my first campaign assignment for Pittsburgh Congressman Rick Santorum's improbable campaign against the incumbent U.S. Senator Harris Wofford. Our opponent was a big deal, a progressive champion, a JFK confidant, and a founder of the Peace Corps. Santorum was the audacious, young conservative, who, along with six others, composed a small band of institutional reformers in Congress who exposed the infamous House Bank Scandal. In 1992, the ethics breach exposed by Santorum and the "Young Turks" led to the resignation or defeat of nearly eighty members of Congress in 1994.

It was the match that lit a revolution.

A few years prior when I was a college freshman, my government professor announced a list of upcoming internships. The following semester, I returned home and was making the daily commute to Senator Rick Santorum's new Pittsburgh office, performing intern duties for no salary but with plenty of enthusiasm.

To me, Santorum was unlike any politician I'd ever met. He exceeded the hype. The man, the motive, and the message all came together in the gutsy, plain language of working people.

My hopes were confirmed early when Tony Fratto—the mild-mannered, smoking, coffee-drinking, suave press secretary to the new senator—waved the staff into his office to see Santorum take on the most visible defender of the old guard, West Virginia's Robert C. Byrd. Santorum was breaking club rules by injecting passion and animated hand motions into typically genteel Senate sessions. To this day, I can't remember the topic, but the vision of my hero drawing his sword against Washington was indelible. With Newt Gingrich and company dismantling the old order in the House of Representatives, our guy was taking on the entire machine in the Senate, one person at a time.

After the internship, my relationship with Santorum and his team remained close, and after my election to the state House, we occasionally hosted joint town hall meetings on federal and state issues or campaigned for rising conservative stars like my soon-to-be neighbor in the legislature, Dave Reed. We were all "giant killers," taking on incumbents and laying out a new philosophical direction for a forgotten part of the state. It was an exhilarating time to be part of the blue-collar Santorum coalition.

The challenge for Santorum was two-fold. First, his positive profile was tied to an unflinching willingness to lay siege to institutions that resisted reform. He was a George Foreman slugger, relentless in his takedowns and often quite effective. His challenge was that he frequently misread the motive behind friendly, rhetorical questions from allies and supportive constituents. In public meetings, he sometimes reversed the premise of a question and prosecuted the questioner. To Rick Santorum, everything was a fight.

The other challenge was that his genuine talent for relationships helped him appreciate the complexities of the people in the Senate. He began to understand that the members of the world's most exclusive club weren't all bad. Many were decent people who in some instances just overstayed, becoming marbleized versions of their former selves. Santorum had a strong capacity for friendship, which included members of leadership, who saw the real value of including the hard-charger on their team. In a twist of irony, he would eventually leave the Senate as a member of leadership, rising to the elected position of Whip—the number-three post. Had he won another term, it is probable that the Majority Leader's spot would have been Santorum's.

The sword-drawing outsider had become a confidant to the ultimate group of insiders. Leadership decisions and responsibilities left little to no room for the reformer to maintain his stance.

Being inside the room created the dual pressures of supporting an independent brand while exercising an insider's influence.

He'd set up an almost impossible standard. When defeat came, at the hands of his personality opposite—the mild-mannered, soft-spoken, Robert P. Casey Jr.—Santorum was again unshackled, and spoiling for a fight.

SANTORUM FOR PRESIDENT

Before Rick Santorum ran for Congress in the early 1990s, as a largely unknown state Senate staffer, he was encouraged to grab a lower rung, something more scalable, like the state House. He ignored the advice, ran and won—defeating an incumbent. Being underrated helped him achieve another statistically impossible feat in the statewide battle against Wofford. Surprise is one of his winning traits. He and his chief political strategist, John Brabender, were master trend spotters, long before the first outliers appeared in the data.

When he ran for president in 2012, instinct and passion, not polling, pulled Santorum up from the back of the pack to the stunning, 34-vote Iowa upset against Mitt Romney. Hard-slogging visits to all the Hawkeye state's 99 counties, often speaking to audiences of a dozen or less, made his story more about grit and tenacity than magic. He'd earned it.

As a former senator with no prospect for an establishment anointing, Santorum ran unencumbered. Against Romney, the scripted, line-tested, perfectly coiffed former Massachusetts governor, Santorum's friendly sweater vest, cowboy boots and "answer everything" strategy was wildly appealing. He didn't hedge on abortion. There was no shifting or surprise position on marriage and family. When confronted with flaws in his record, he'd admit fault and point out his miscalculations. He was the anti-Romney.

When the caucus and primary season ended, surges in small donations and good polling weren't enough to topple the frontrunner. Santorum would enter presidential history in second place, and earn the right to run in 2016 if Romney stumbled.

But in 2016, Donald Trump happened. Santorum's chief attributes as the truth-telling, blue-collar conservative struggled against a better-funded field that had studied the lessons of Santorum 2012. Each competitor, including Trump, embraced their own brand, and self-appointed themselves champions for the American worker. In one of the great ironies of American politics, a billionaire became the people's voice.

SANTORUM AT CORNELL: A CONTROLLED FIRE

Eventually, progressive groups began to sketch a cartoon version of Rick Santorum as the pugnacious, Catholic culture warrior obsessed with gay marriage and abortion. Knowing his willingness to engage the most strident opponents, he became the target of almost weekly attacks from the outer rings of the blogosphere, including a campaign to make his last name synonymous with lewd sex acts. The latter took years of technological wizardry to overcome.

Now and then, the public would see past the cutout to the real Rick Santorum, a man transformed by faith and strengthened through trials. When he and his wife, Karen, lost their infant son Gabriel, and later announced a public suspension of Santorum's 2012 campaign to be at the side of his youngest daughter, Bella, during a life-threatening episode, Santorum's true identity shined. To unfamiliar reporters and debate stage partners who observed him under pressure, the purported, single-issue culture warrior became "Rick"—someone altogether unlike his caricature.

In his current role as an at-large ambassador for the full spectrum of conservative policies, Santorum has accepted invitations to university campuses well outside the comfort zone of his Catholic and evangelical Christian fan base. In speeches at Brown, Harvard, Penn, Yale and Cornell, he has relished the role of missionary.

When I spoke with him by phone in early December, he had just left the Senate floor on a rare visit to the old jobsite. I asked him about his goal in entering the unwelcoming territory of the Ivy League. His answer applied to campus talks as well as frequent appearances on left-of-center networks like CNN and MSNBC.

"I know that I'm reaching people that will never hear this message in a way that's thoughtful and hopefully compelling. Not threatening, not moralizing, not judgmental, but simply exposing people to reason," he explains. "For most conservatives speaking to a college campus, it's their shtick to incite," he observes. "You don't engage people intellectually."

The aim of communication, he argues, is to persuade, not provoke. "If you can take their cage down, and allow them to receive some of what you're saying, there's a tremendous opportunity," he says.

Is this a changed Rick Santorum, or is this a fuller picture of the same man? The answer is both.

"That fire is still there. I'm obviously very passionate about the things I believe in," he assures me. The difference, he contends, is stepping back from the practice of putting opponents on trial. His goal now is to make the case in a way that opens minds, asking, "Why would you be angry with people who are ill-informed, or in most cases have been lied to?" Paraphrasing one of his favorite sayings about persuasion, he says, "People don't care what you think until they think you care."

It's an acknowledgment that extends to one of his passion points, the dignity of all human life, especially the unborn and disabled. The old tactics of the pro-life movement trafficked heavily in shock and condemnation. The result was not mass conversion to his pro-life views, but revulsion.

"What we found out is that there were millions of women out there who were hurting, and all we were doing was judging them, instead of helping them and loving them." When dialogue is about understanding and changing lives, he says, "of course they'll listen to people who care about them, instead of people who will just judge them. Nobody wants to be judged."

More than 2,000 attendees packed a meeting of the Yale Political Union to hear Santorum defend the resolution that "the federal government is destroying the American family." The two-and-a-half-hour engagement, like many of Santorum's forays into public discourse, highlighted the fact that most students hadn't heard a reasoned, hopeful, conservative message. Their only exposure had come through the voices of provocateurs and showmen. It's a phenomenon Santorum understands well.

"I'm in a unique position because I blew up the town square for a long time, and people show up to see me because they think I'm going to blow up the town square again," he reflects, adding that "they either show up in protest or curiosity."

But time has tempered the warrior instincts. Prosecuting is no longer his first instinct in conversation. "It's taken me a long time to learn it. I still have my moments where I probably go a little to far, but I always try to remember that this generation as been lied to." While he doesn't support the view that students are victims, he acknowledges that this is likely their first real exposure to viewpoints like his.

During a widely circulated December 2016 speech at Cornell University, Santorum faced a crowd of approximately 500. Throughout his talk, a small contingent of hecklers attempted to drown out the former senator, crying "Shame, shame, shame!"

Unrattled and calm, Santorum refused to take the bait but engaged in a thoughtful dialogue about the public square and the need to preserve open space for opposing views. Unlike other times, there was no detectable anger or disgusted smirk, just the wise, seasoned response of a more gracious communicator.

What is the lesson in all of this, I ask? He responds, "You can't engage people if the volume is too high or the tongue is too sharp." No unconverted liberal is going to listen to a hell-raising conservative. "Sometimes we think we have nothing to learn," he continues. "That's not true."

The result of Santorum's outreach into hostile territory isn't always obvious. This time it was. Santorum forwarded the following note from a Cornell student:

Dear Senator Santorum,

Firstly, and above all else, I would like to thank you for coming to speak at Cornell. I understand, both before and now especially after your talk, that such an appearance was not easy. It says a lot about your character that you came to speak your mind in an environment that you likely knew would not be receptive of much of what you had to say.

Your talk was an inspiration to me, and I wanted to tell you why.

You surprised me by walking onto a stage, in front of a booing crowd, and opening a dialogue. Your first words were in advocacy of open-mindedness and a constructive conversation. You extended an olive branch in an environment that had already treated you unfairly, and continued to hold it out even as you were screamed at and called names.

Regardless of the differences in our viewpoints, that was inspiring. You handled the harsh, immature, and hateful interruptions of your speech with grace and admirable composure. Listening to that, albeit small, group of protesters try to aggressively silence your views was alarming (certainly not very democratic), and I share many of their viewpoints. . . .

Even as I write this I find it hard to fully articulate the impact your visit had on me. We agree on very little, but your character and the manner in which you conducted yourself re-opened my mind in less than two hours. I cannot thank you enough for that. I wanted to tell you all of this because I hope that knowing that you were able to inspire that in me, and I hope not just me, overshadows the attacks and disruptions and reassures you that your visit meant something.

I also hope it further encourages you to continue holding out the olive branch, even to your most passionate opposition. It is my hope that doing so will cause more and more people to reach back, giving our country a chance to come together in this time of divisiveness and tense polarity.

–unnamed student, Cornell University Class of 2019

In his courageous, lengthy journey in public life, Santorum has refused to disengage, even when he's been miscast or misunderstood. He understands the art of long-form oratory and personal engagement is giving way to a culture of memes and emoticons. The town square he's now constructively trying to rebuild is struggling against the emotional shallowness of social media.

"We've become actually more isolated from each other as a result of technology than more aware of each other," he warns. "You can go and get all your news from your selected, preferred sites that reinforce everything you believe in—you just don't interact with other thought."

Over time, Rick Santorum and those of us who've followed closely behind have conceded the need for our manners and methods to more fully reflect the idea that those opposite us are not enemies, but people made in the image of God, deserving all the dignity and respect that distinction affords.

Civility is worth the fight.

Courage isn't brashness or bravado, it's recognition that without humility we have nothing important to say.

Courage informed by faith in God allows us to risk reputation and stand for the sake of loving others.

Courage can often be found in serenity and silence more than the trumpets of self-promotion.

Hon. John B. McCue, Hon. C. Doyle Steele
Photos: Official Photographs | PA House of Representatives

CHAPTER SIX

SOLUTIONS

Re-humanizing American Politics & Public Discourse

Doyle Steele and John McCue recited three significant oaths in their lifetimes. The first was a vow to their wives in Christian marriage. The second was a commitment to their country as volunteers during World War II. The third was their installation vows as elected members of the Pennsylvania House of Representatives in the 60s and 70s.

By the time my life intersected with theirs, both were old men. Their marriages were still vibrant, but their service in war and politics was rarely, if ever, mentioned. The medals and primetime achievements were all but forgotten by their communities. They were men of action, defined by quietly keeping their word. Commitment was paramount.

When both agreed to chair my campaign for state representative, it was a somewhat unusual pairing. John was a noted Republican and prominent attorney. Doyle or "Abe," as he was known, was a Kennedy

Democrat who once shared a platform with JFK during a campaign stop in Western Pennsylvania.

What made the duo even more unlikely is that they were once competitors for the same job. In 1972 McCue defeated the incumbent Steele for the same legislative seat I would hold decades later. I never heard either man express negativity about the contest or their opponent. Service in war or government wasn't brag-worthy, it was the duty they both shouldered.

LEARNING FROM THE MILITARY

If we're looking for men and women who exhibit the same willingness to service, we should take a look at veterans.

Gabe Stultz is a longtime friend and decorated former first lieutenant in the 101st Airborne Division who served as infantry platoon leader in Afghanistan. After completing his military commitment, he went on to earn a law degree from Wake Forest University and is now a lobbyist for the Paralyzed Veterans of America.

When I ask Stultz about those he commanded, he describes the post-war tragedy of men he loves. Many of his guys "fell into traps" because of the abrupt end to their service and the loss of a cause greater than themselves. Injuries combined with a purposeless reentry into civilian life kept many veterans from finding their next mission.

For many of these men, he argues, public service could be an ideal second career for the following reasons:

> 1. Because they've experienced active, aggressive resistance to their military missions, veterans are well-acclimated to adversity.
>
> 2. Veterans are prepared to complete assignments and missions with minimal to no guidance or instruction.
>
> 3. Veterans are trained to resolve problems creatively, without delay or excuse.

The last characteristic might be the most useful in trying to make dysfunctional government work. "They don't need their hands held. Give them a task, and they will find a way to do it," says Stultz. I think he's right.

But as old-world virtues begin to disappear in the civilian world, can military traditions and history keep their institutions intact? Will the same cultural pressures that are devastating civil discourse and public debate prevent military men and women from pursuing elective office?

For perspective, I turned to another close friend who held senior positions in the United States Air Force Judge Advocate

General's Corps, including a tour of duty supporting Operation Enduring Freedom missions in Kyrgyzstan. Davis Younts served as Chief of the Military Justice Division of the Air Force's JAG school and designed the criminal law and trial advocacy training program.

As both defense counsel and senior prosecutor, Younts has seen comrades demonstrate the capacity for the noble and despicable. He expresses concern about the increasing pressure on military leaders to complete assignments and preserve opportunities for promotion. He argues that increasingly aggressive performance timetables have caused some essential military values to fragment. The notion of honor, as an example, is too often giving way to civilian-style pragmatism and expediency.

"There is a huge incentive to check a box, run checklists and fudge numbers," he argues. In the military, you have "a very short window of opportunity" to prove your readiness for promotion. The military, Younts argues, must be on guard against the deterioration of personal values. The presence of high-responsibility jobs and performance awards does not necessarily correspond with honorable action.

"I don't think you can ignore changes in society and the shifting priorities of honor and respect," says Younts. The revolution of values has impacted institutions across the board.

Still, the military's overall example may provide an argument against waging political campaigns without a standard for truth, respect, and decorum.

"The American military has always tried to live by the Articles of War because there is an idea that how you wage war governs the conditions of the peace," says Younts. "If you wage a total war on the civilian population of a country, you destroy any possibility for meaningful and lasting peace."

It makes sense to apply this same principle to the present breakdown in political civility, he argues. When candidates wage ruthless, scorched-earth campaigns against people of opposing ideas, says Younts, "it undermines the trust that the American people have in their institutions."

THE FACE OF CIVILITY

Still, electing a wave of men and women of proven ability and character to public office won't resolve the present crisis in our public discourse. Selecting a new type of leader requires a consensus, one that says we expect more from the people we elevate to leadership. Holding candidates to high standards of civility and public conduct is the citizen's responsibility.

All of this is, at best, hopeful idealism. It's not the take-a-pill-and-call-me-in-the-morning answer we've been hunting since the beginning of the 2016 election process. We're in deep trouble, and we know it. The 50/50 American divide isn't going to work much longer.

I've concluded that the answer isn't a political one. Manners derive from motives. Motives flow from a place that cannot be governed by external rewards or punishments—the human heart. So, while we can't put 2016 back in the bottle, we can learn from those who have resisted the mob. Some of these role models have lived in different eras, but many are already occupying the spaces where we live and work. Why are they at peace? Why do they refuse to allow anxiety and fear to spill out in anger on Facebook or at the Thanksgiving table? How do they read the same headlines, but operate in a stable, even-keeled, grace-filled manner?

The answer is that we are all created by a loving God who demands something more than mere tolerance. His standard is much higher than the easy slogans of civility. Love, respect, and humility—this is his standard for life and elections.

I'll close with a prayer my pastor, Brett Hartman, offered in the days before the presidential election of 2016. Our church, like yours perhaps, was experiencing many of the same heightened tensions of the impending decision. His prayer is also mine for this season in American history and beyond:

> Father, I think we have to admit—I think I have to admit—that it is so easy to take sides. I pray that you would help us as your people to grow absolutely sick and tired of taking sides.

That we would not take the pinnacle of your Creation and treat it like trash because of opposing opinions. That we would be about the process of re-humanizing those around us—treating them with the dignity that you gave them—because you have created us in your image.

God, I pray that your people would be civil and polite. That they would speak truth with there is truth, even when it comes to a contentious and ugly presidential election.

Father, I thank you for the truths that you have given us—and there are truths, and we hold to them. Each one of us has beliefs about how you will help this society to grow and to flourish, but help us to not hold onto these beliefs at the expense of the people you have created.

God help us to remember: Is there anyone who is better? No, none, none at all. May we fear you. May we walk in the blessing of the Gospel you have given us.

In Jesus' name, Amen.

Thank you for reading. Email me at jeff@churchillmedia.org if you'd like to continue the conversation. I'd love to hear from you.

ABOUT THE AUTHORS

NORRIS CLARK | FOREWORD

R. Norris Clark is the Managing Partner of Princeton Strategic Communications, helping a talented team of communicators to tell the stories of good companies and causes.

Before starting Princeton Strategic Communications, he was appointed by the NJ State Board of Education to open the Family and Community Relations Office. For several years he promoted the Jersey Shore including Wildwood and Cape May, helping clients win the NJ Governor's Tourism Award.

Upon seeing Ross Perot on television in 1992, his wife (a Wall Street veteran) challenged him to do something about the national debt, which led him to help Perot form a two-million-member national advocacy organization for government reform. At the encouragement of Perot, he made marketing communications his career and joined Perot Systems, specializing first in Customer Relationship Management (CRM) serving Saks Fifth Avenue, then in Telecom serving AT&T, and finally in Financial Services serving UBS.

Clark organizes TEDxCapeMay and, until recently, served as the Deputy Mayor for his hometown.

JEFF COLEMAN | AUTHOR, WITH ALL DUE RESPECT

For over two decades, Jeff Coleman has served hundreds of individuals and causes. From designing brand identities and communications plans to leading community-wide discussions on organizational culture and idea formation, his aim is to be a joyful help to everyone he encounters. You'll often find him on the Amtrak Keystone Line—commuting between offices in Harrisburg and Trenton.

Jeff is a former member of the Pennsylvania House of Representatives, borough councilman in his hometown of Apollo, Pennsylvania, and radio newscaster on WLNI-FM in Lynchburg, VA. He often cites another trio of jobs as the most meaningful: waiting tables at the Main Street Eatery in Lynchburg, Virginia; cleaning rooms at the Roadway Inn in Kittanning, Pennsylvania; and stocking shelves at the former Oliver's IGA in Apollo.

The son of Presbyterian missionary parents, he spent many of his formative years in his mother's homeland of the Republic of the Philippines. He maintains a strong interest in maintaining the longstanding commitment between the United States and the Philippine people.

Jeff and his wife, Rebecca, live in Lemoyne, Pennsylvania with their four young children, Anna, Teddy, Charlotte and Henry. The Colemans are active members of New Covenant Fellowship of the greater Harrisburg area.

SOURCES

CHAPTER 1
- *Gallup Presidential Leadership Poll*, March 2016.
- Tros-dale Idea Began on Blue Ridge, *(Charlottesville Daily Progress)*, October 1, 1968.

CHAPTER 2
- Francis Martel, Philippine's Duterte Congratulates Donald Trump *(Breitbart)*, November 9, 2016.
- *Mason's Manual of Legislative Procedure* (various citations).

CHAPTER 3
- President Theodore Roosevelt, dedication speech at the Pennsylvania State Capitol, Harrisburg, (www.theodore-roosevelt.com), October 4, 1906.
- George Skelton, California Republicans have nowhere to go but up — and Assemblyman Chad Mayes could be the one to lead them there *(Los Angeles Times)*, December 19, 2016.
- Chad Mayes, A call for a return to politics with true civility *(Desert Sun)*, November 11, 2016.

CHAPTER 4
- President Richard Nixon, National Association of Broadcasters Convention, Houston, (www.presidency.ucsb.edu), March 19, 1974.
- *NBC News/Wall Street Journal Poll* (*Meet the Press*, January 1, 2016).

ACKNOWLEDGEMENTS

I want to express heartfelt gratitude to the teams at Churchill Creative and Princeton Strategic Communications for their enthusiasm and encouragement to begin and complete this book. Specific thanks to friends Amy Kulling, Donna Ceperich, and Corey Graham for accepting the added burdens of this project, and to Scott Cole for the forbearance he extended throughout the ambitious design process. The book would not have happened without Scotty's grace and creativity.

My new friend and able editor, Rachel Stout, brought clarity and brevity to an overflow of thoughts. I'm grateful for her many contributions. Any mistakes that remain are mine alone.

Beyond beautiful photographs, my brother Joel Coleman contributed a contagious love and respect for the people we encountered. He's a joyful partner. Also in the picture department, appreciation is due to my best pal and gifted photographer, Bill Crawford, for partnering on this project and in the daily calling to follow Jesus.

Thanks to my good friend, Frank Weiss at Princeton Strategic Communications and Lynne Goldstein, a longtime associate at Goldstein Photography in Pittsburgh, for capturing the moment with Dan

Rather. Frank's film work and Lynn's photographs added immeasurably to this project.

Nothing can adequately convey the depth of my appreciation and respect for Norris Clark, and the joy of serving alongside someone who continually gives more than he receives. He, Carolinn, Karen, Emaleigh, Amy, Frank and my other PSC colleagues are professionals without peer, and true friends.

Finally, my heart is overflowing with thankfulness to my wife Rebecca for keeping the life and laughter of our home from being overwhelmed by the arrival of this project, and many seasons of others. Without her heart, I would never have understood the love and contentment that comes from being her husband and dad to Anna, Teddy, Charlotte and Henry. It's a wonderful life.